Has
The New Liturgy
Changed
You?

Has
The New Liturgy
Changed
You?

by

Mary Perkins Ryan

PAULIST PRESS DEUS BOOKS

NEW YORK   GLEN ROCK   WESTMINSTER
TORONTO   AMSTERDAM

NIHIL OBSTAT:
Rev. James J. O'Connor
Censor Librorum

IMPRIMATUR:
✠Leo A. Pursley, D.D.
Bishop of Fort Wayne-South Bend
December 3, 1966

The Nihil Obstat and Imprimatur are official declarations that a book or pamphlet is free of doctrinal or moral error. No implication is contained therein that those who have granted the Nihil Obstat and Imprimatur agree with the contents, opinions or statements expressed.

Library of Congress
Catalog Card Number: 67-15721

Cover Design: Morris Berman

Published by Paulist Press
Editorial Office: 304 W. 58th St., N.Y., N.Y. 10019
Business Office: Glen Rock, New Jersey 07452

Printed in the
United States of America
by Our Sunday Visitor Press

Contents

IV

PRAISE AND SACRIFICE: THE GREAT EUCHARISTIC PRAYER AND SACRIFICE

V

COMMUNION RITES FROM THE "OUR FATHER" TO THE END OF MASS

VI

A BEGINNING, NOT AN ACHIEVEMENT

Foreword

Few Catholics seem to be happy with the present Mass. When it is poorly done, even the most ardent reformer would prefer to be back in the days of the silent Latin Mass. When it is well done, it cries out for a really drastic reappraisal. We are halfway between a form of the Mass conceived and carried out as a mysterious sacred action which needn't make sense, and forms in which real people today could find and express the Christian meaning of their lives as they gather together to celebrate the Lord's supper. Such a neither-here-nor-there situation cannot be a comfortable or satisfactory one.

Yet the present unhappiness is not only due to the existing inadequate — and in many ways meaningless — Mass rite. One can endure a lot of discomfort on a journey if he knows where he is going. But too many Catholics have not effectively been informed as to what the changes in the liturgy were all about, what direction they are indicating for Christian worship and Christian life. The *Constitution on the Sacred Liturgy* insists that "liturgical education" be given to clergy and laity alike, but rare is the bishop or pastor who has seriously undertaken this task.

This collection of articles, originally published in a weekly column in several Catholic papers, is one attempt to meet this need. It will serve its purpose if it in any way helps its readers to see the changes in the

Mass (and in the Church) as signs of life, so that they can get with them and then move forward to a more truly living worship of the living God.

MARY PERKINS RYAN

I
THE "NEW STYLE"
IN WORSHIP

New-Style
Masses

A couple we know live in a diocese where "new style" Masses became the rule some time before 1964. After spending three weeks in another diocese during their vacation, they reported to their pastor back home, "Sunday Mass up there seemed very strange. So silent and sort of hurried. The congregation didn't say anything except the prayers after Mass. Nobody even read the epistle and Gospel in English. We didn't feel as if we had really been to Mass at all." And the pastor remarked, "Don't you remember last winter when we started participation here? You people were the first to complain that you didn't like all the singing and praying out loud. You said *that* didn't seem like a real Mass."

So those who are distressed about the present changes in the liturgy and the thought of more changes in the future can take heart. When they get used to the new way of doing things, maybe they will like it.

But, of course, simply getting used to one change or another is not the whole problem. No one of the present "new" practices is really so very new. There has always been some English in the liturgy — in baptism and marriage, for instance; now there will be more. The Church has been asking for more active participation, in one way or another, from the time of St. Pius X. Even celebrating Mass facing the people isn't an innovation in the Church; the main altars of some of the great basilicas in Rome were built that way many centuries ago.

What upsets people, devout people particularly perhaps, is not any one change, but the thought that the Church is changing and asking them to change accustomed ways of thinking and acting. This seems a very disturbing idea. In our modern world, religion has seemed the one area of life we could count on to stay *un*changed.

Such people are quite right in realizing that the Church is changing — not as to essentials, but in thinking out afresh and realizing in daily life what the essentials really mean. But this is something to be happy about, not afraid of. For many reasons, the Church has seemed unchanging in the last centuries, but this is not her normal state. She has to change to remain herself, and to be to changing mankind what Christ means her to be. And we have to change if we are to be truly alive as Christians. Changelessness is not a property of living things. And so it is certainly good news, not bad, that we belong to a living Church.

In recent centuries — due in part to the unnatural "changelessness" of the Church during this period — religion has come to seem increasingly divorced from human thinking and living. When Catholics went to Mass, for instance, they didn't expect to act like real people, but as much as possible like disembodied souls. And, equally, they didn't suspect that what they did at Mass was meant to affect what they did outside —

for example, how they treated members of minority groups.

One main purpose of the present renewal, then, is to help us become more fully human in our religious affairs and more fully religious in our human affairs, so that our lives will be wholly human and wholly Christian, closer at once to God and to our fellowmen. We surely cannot be unhappy at such a prospect, even if it means discarding some of cherished religious notions to take on truer ones, and changing some of our cherished ways to take on better ones.

In this light, we shall discuss some of the changes both in thinking and in acting called for, and implied by, the *Constitution on the Sacred Liturgy,* to see what their purposes are and why they can be welcomed as truly good news.

A Chance
To Grow Up

A psychiatrist friend of ours once made an informal survey to find out Catholics' motives for going to Sunday Mass. He stood by the door of his suburban parish church after Mass one Sunday morning and asked his acquaintances as they emerged, "Why did you come to Mass?" The great majority said, "Because we have to; it's the law of the Church." A few said, "Because it makes me feel good." And one of these turned on our friend and asked, "Why do *you* come to Mass?" He answered, rather timidly, "Well, to worship God." And the other man exclaimed, "Tom, you are one in a million!"

This incident shows very clearly one of the reasons why a renewal is needed in our worship. If most Catholics consider the weekly participation in the central act of their religion as primarily the fulfillment of an obligation, or a way to "feel good," then something is wrong. For these are childish motives, not those of mature persons. Children can't appreciate the real reasons for doing many of the things they should do. They have to be forced to do them by definite laws and fear of the consequences of disobedience, or coaxed to do them by tangible rewards. Are we too immature religiously to understand the real reasons for going to Mass?

What are these reasons? The *Constitution on the Sacred Liturgy* says, "To praise God in the midst of his Church, to take part in the sacrifice, and to eat the Lord's supper." Again, in more detail, to "be instructed by God's Word and nourished at the table of the Lord's body; to give thanks to God; by offering the immaculate victim . . . to learn to offer themselves; through Christ the mediator, to be drawn day by day into ever more perfect union with God and with each other, so that finally God may be all in all." In short, to worship God as only Christians can do.

All of us are certainly capable of understanding what it is we go to Mass to do. Even a child can realize something of what it is to praise God, to learn from him, to offer him a gift, to be close to him and to other people in love. . . . But one great difficulty has been that what we actually did at Mass didn't seem very much like praising or offering. Simply kneeling or sitting in silence, for instance, hardly seems like "praising God in the midst of his Church." Silently thronging up to the communion rail doesn't seem in the least like eating a supper.

The present changes in the way we take part in the Mass are, then, in the direction of helping us to *realize* what we are meant to be doing at Mass and to *do* it — not as disembodied souls, but as whole human persons and members of a community. Singing hymns, saying prayers of praise out loud, sitting down to hear God's Word, exchanging greetings with the celebrant and saying "Amen" to the prayers he offers in our name —

all these actions express our part in the various phases of the Mass and so help us to understand it and take it.

And the future changes in the way Mass is celebrated will help still more. As the *Constitution on the Sacred Liturgy* says, "Both texts and rites are to be drawn up so that they express more clearly the holy things which they signify; the Christian people, so far as possible, should be enabled to understand with ease and to take part in them fully, actively and as befits a community."

It is surely good news, then, that the Church is now giving us a fresh opportunity to become mature Christians. If we welcome it and use it, we may hope that a future survey of why Catholics go to Sunday Mass will show that we have "put aside childish things" and "grown up in Christ."

Religion
Is for Now

When I was young, I wrote a book of useful information for converts about life in the Church. It was accepted by a publisher, and I was pleased with it and with myself. I had the manuscript back home for some final revisions, when Fr. H. A. Reinhold, one of the great liturgical pioneers, happened to come to see us. He picked up my precious manuscript and opened it to the section about the liturgical year. I had said that during Advent the Church relived the time before our Lord's birth, and that Advent was four weeks long because it used to be thought that only four thousand years had gone by between Adam and Christ. "Where did you learn that stuff?" Fr. Reinhold asked. "Why, we were taught it in school," I said defensively. "Now listen. . . ." he said.

I had to change all that part of my book. But it was a thousand times worth the effort to be given my first glimpse into the vast effort of modern scriptural, liturgical and doctrinal scholarship to bring us back to the realities of Christian faith and life, where these had become obscured by mis-emphases in thinking or in practice.

The trouble with the time-before-Christ notion of Advent, as with other pious "traditions" not founded on liturgical or scriptural or doctrinal truth, is that it makes religion seem unreal, an escape from reality rather than the way to it. In this case, the urgency of the Advent call to "make straight the way of the Lord" here and now, by furthering justice, love and peace in ourselves and our families and our communities and our world — this passes us by completely if we think that during Advent we are supposed to try to live in some other age than our own.

The truth is almost precisely the opposite, as any alert reading of the Advent Masses shows. One purpose of Advent is to help us realize precisely where we are in time, in human history, so that we can act accordingly. We are living in the age *after* Christ's coming to mankind by taking on our human nature and being born in Bethlehem; the age in which he *is continually coming* to us, in the Church and in our neighbor — and coming to all men through us; the age in which we *look forward to his coming* in glory at the end of time.

The "let's pretend" idea of Advent could only have grown up in a time when Catholics had largely forgotten the wonderful truth restated in the *Constitution on the Sacred Liturgy:* "Christ is present in his Word, since it is he himself who speaks when the holy scriptures are read in the Church." Through the texts of the Advent Masses — whether they are from St. Paul's letters about life in the Church, or from the gospels about the end of the world or the work of St. John the Baptist, or lessons or songs from the Old Testament — Christ is speaking to us here and now. He wants to alert us to his coming to us *now.* He is urging us to help prepare ourselves and all mankind to welcome him now and at the end of time. He is not giving us a history lesson, or even a sacred history lesson, but showing us, *through* what people did or should have done to prepare for his coming to mankind, what we should be doing now.

But, of course, it was hard to realize that Christ was really speaking to us in the liturgy — let alone telling us things of vital import for our daily living — when the priest had to proclaim his message facing a wall and in Latin. Now, the direct use of our own language will allow Christ's Word more effectively to reach our hearts and minds — if we let it — to form us as real Christians, of today.

God-with-Us

The New Yorker, I think it was, reported one year recently around Christmas time that, when two ladies stopped to look at a nativity scene set up in a department-store window, one of them complained to the other, "Religion is getting into everything these days. They're even trying to take over Christmas!"

This incident might seem to show the need for renewed efforts to "bring Christ back into Christmas" by promoting more carol singing and less "Jingle Bells," more cards depicting the nativity and fewer showing Scottish terriers, etc. But I do not think that it does, unless we realize what the purpose of such things is. Otherwise, we may be contributing to the present widespread conviction that religion is a sedative to keep weak people from facing real life.

St. Francis, we are told, set up the first Christmas crib, giving a powerful impetus to "realistic" representations of the nativity. But his purpose was to give those who looked at it a new realization of the great love of the Son of God for men — the love that caused him to become man for us and to be born in a stable and laid in a manger in such poverty and helplessness

— so that they might be moved to amend their lives and live like true Christians.

If we kept this purpose in mind, we would surely throw out a great deal of the current slick Christmas "art." And we also might begin to clarify a confusion in our minds which may prevent us from seeing clearly what Christmas is all about. We are, certainly, meant to think about our Lord's birthday at Bethlehem and to meditate on all its circumstances. But we are not called upon to think that Christ himself becomes a baby every year at Christmas.

It is true that the living and glorious Christ, God and man, is now all that he was in the various stages of his earthly life. It is true that, in the sacrifice of the Mass, the whole "work of our redemption is renewed." Theologians discuss at length the once-for-all character of the events of our Lord's life on earth and their enduring relevance to our "now."

But the notion that, for example, "the baby Jesus is coming into your heart" at your Christmas communion confuses us about the reality and actuality of our personal relationship with the Lord. In order to understand and love her husband better, a wife might look at pictures of her husband's childhood and think about things that had happened to him. But she would be extremely upset if he *became* a child. We don't "relate" to a child as we do to a mature person. (Children, particularly, are confused by "the baby Jesus." It is the grown-up Jesus, the same all the year round, whom they want as their friend.)

And the danger is that if we think of the Lord as being a baby now, we shall think that he only asks of us what a baby asks — warm affection and attention — whereas the living and glorified Lord who is present with us in the Church wants us to know him as a Person, to respond to his invitation to share his life, his plans, his work.

The Constitution on the Sacred Liturgy is, therefore, again directing us toward reality when it states that the Christ who was born and died and rose again is always present in his Church: in the sacrifice of the Mass, in the sacraments, in his Word, whenever the Church prays and sings. And he himself has told us that he is present in our neighbor.

If we want to "bring Christ back into Christmas" — or, much better, if we want to proclaim the good news that God is really with us — we need to become more aware of, and responsive to, his presence among us in all these ways. Then religion will be getting into everything indeed, not as a cosy glow of vague goodwill, but as the fire Christ came to cast upon the earth.

Why Social Worship?

Last year, my husband taught the CCD course for high school juniors and seniors in our parish — a small group on which various approaches had been tried and none with much success. He decided to read with them, discussing as they went, Fr. Louis Bouyer's *Introduction to the Spiritual Life* — a book designed, one might think, not only for an older but also for a more "spiritual" audience. They never got beyond the first chapter, but the students kept coming to class all through the year. For the readings and discussion opened out to them a new idea of religion: that God wants to have a real relationship with each of us, that he speaks to us personally through his incarnate Word, his Son, that we can really come to know him in the Church.

Every Catholic, indeed, who already is alive to this "I-Thou" relationship, as modern philosophers call it, with Christ our Lord, made possible for us in the Church, treasures it as the heart of his religious life. He doesn't want anything to interfere with it or endanger it. And he is often afraid that this is just what the Church's call to "social worship" is going to do. Won't this regimentation at Mass do away with the personal character of his prayer? How can he speak with the Lord after communion, for instance, if he has to be singing a hymn?

This is an objection to the "new-style" Mass that cannot just be brushed away. One answer is that we can pray as we like on other occasions; when we come to Mass, we come together as the People of God to pray to him as a community. But this doesn't really solve the problem. Devout people want to know: how can I find Christ in this new kind of Mass as I used to in the old one, when I was left alone to pray my own way?

The answer is that they can find a far more complete companionship with Christ by taking part in the "new-style" Mass than they did in the old. For now we can more easily know him and be with him in *all* the signs through which he gives and reveals himself to us in the Mass. And the first of these is, precisely, the *other people* whom we are asked not only to kneel beside, but to sing and listen and pray and offer *with*.

Christ is present, the *Constitution on the Sacred Liturgy says,* "whenever the Church prays and sings, for he promised, 'Where two or three are gathered together in my name, there am I in the midst of you.'" And so, we are with Christ in a special way at Mass first because we are members of this congregation. The very fact that all these people have come together in his name is a guarantee of his presence among us.

And therefore we cannot be less close to him, but rather more so, when we allow ourselves to be aware of all the other people at Mass; when we think of them and ourselves as "we" — the "we" who have come to be with Christ; when we sing and listen and pray and offer with them. St. John tells us that "we know that we have passed from death to life *because* we love the brethren." It would be very odd, then, if the companionship of our brethren in any way separated us from the companionship of Christ!

One difficulty is, of course, that we have never thought of the Mass as in any way meant to be the kind of *human* affair the Last Supper was — a gathering of friends, a celebration. What we try to feel — and often do feel — at Christmas celebrations, namely the happiness of being together in God's love, is the kind of feeling we should have at every Sunday Mass. And the present changes are in this direction — to help us be more at one with one another, and so more at one with Christ.

Why Sing at Mass?

Last summer, to find out more about what our older boys are so interested in, we watched the weekly hootenanny on TV every Saturday night. Who says that Americans don't like to sing anymore? Doubters might object that it is only teen-agers who do; you'll never get older people singing. But last year I took part in the annual luncheon of a Catholic women's organization in a midwestern diocese and heard some twenty-four hundred women — all beyond, and many well beyond, the teen-age bracket — almost raising the roof singing "Happy Birthday" to one of their moderators. And, at the liturgical week every year, thousands of men and women joined in singing at the Masses, and as many hundreds as could crowd into the halls went to sing with Fr. Rivers, who composed the *American Mass Program,* and at what were called "Hymnannys."

So the idea that Americans, or American Catholics, as such don't like to sing is simply not true. But there certainly are a great many of us who don't like the idea of singing at Mass — of singing ourselves, that is, along with all the other members of the congregation

18

who, like ourselves, may or may not have good voices. What is the value of our singing that a choir can't achieve for us?

It is certainly a normal human instinct to sing whenever people get together for any kind of a celebration — an instinct pretty well inhibited in many New Englanders, perhaps, but generally found in all races and cultures all over the world. For singing unites persons in action, action involving their whole selves. It at once helps to create unity among persons and to express it. In singing, the lonely find companionship, the isolated break out of their shells — as you can see if you watch the faces of people taking part in hootenannys.

Now, we Catholics need this great means of community-building at Mass if we are to realize our companionship with Christ and one another. The power of the eucharist to make us "all one body, who eat of the one bread" is frustrated if we are shut up in ourselves, cut off from one another. Singing at Mass — not all the time, of course, but at least at the beginning and end, and, above all, at communion time — can't make us into Christians who truly love one another, but it can bring home to us some of the requirements and the joys of our unity in Christ. It is, at least potentially, a very powerful means of helping us to be whole human persons at Mass, persons who find joy in being and acting with other persons in the love of Christ.

Of course, it may take some time before the singing in your parish church seems anything like a sign of unity. It may take a much longer time before hymns are composed that really suit the requirements of religious singing today, both in words and music. It must raise our hearts and minds to God — but *our* hearts and minds, not those of people of some other time and place. It must unite us, not simply as a cheerful human gathering, but as members of Christ. It must help us to worship more fully, to worship as Christians. These are not easy requirements for poets and musicians to meet.

But we shall never get anywhere by not singing the best hymns that are available today — singing them as best we can, trying to sing better, the better to "praise God in the Church."

Do We Have To Be
Active at Mass Too?

"I rush around the house all week and only get out for some parish or community activity. On Saturday I have the car, so I do all the shopping and get the children to the dentist and scout meetings and all that while my husband does the odd jobs at home. Sunday morning is a rush, getting the children ready for church. The way things used to be, when I got to Mass I could relax and just be peaceful with God for forty-five minutes. Now they've taken this away from me too. We have to sing and say responses and be on the ball all the time. Sunday Mass seems like just one more chore."

This is the suburban-mother-with-young-children variety of the complaint many Catholics are now making. People went to Mass for peace and quiet with God and they aren't finding it any longer. Is the answer to their problem simply, "Don't worry. When you get used to the new ways you will be able to relax just the way you used to?" It is certainly true that the worry and confusion which go with new ways of doing things will gradually disappear. We won't have to be anxious about when to get up and sit down. The singing will improve and, we may hope, begin to be a source of joy and not distraction. If we are trying to think and feel with the Church, we shall be able to find even greater *peacefulness* at Mass than we used to. But we can never go back to the old *passivity*.

For, if taking part in the Mass is to be a living force in our very active lives, taking part in it must be active too — not in the sense of hurry of busyness, but of using our human powers. We do not go to Mass for the reason that we take our cars to the gas station, to be pumped full of grace for another week. God treats us like human persons, not like things. He wants us to go to Mass to meet with Christ, to hear him, to respond with him to the Father's love by offering his sacrifice of praise, to be united with him and one another by eating the bread that makes us one body. By taking part with our minds and hearts and wills and voices and bodies in these holy "activities," we are renewed and revitalized for another week of "hearing the Word of God and putting it into practice."

There are, certainly, periods in our lives when the only possible form of "recreation" — the only thing we feel can really recreate us — is just to sit and rest. But this is not the normal way, even in the busiest of lives. We usually seek recreation in a change of activity — in skiing or swimming of talking or dancing — not in just sitting. And so we can be recreated and refreshed for Christian living by taking part actively in the Mass — by singing and listening and praying and offering and receiving in and with our parish community. As we all know, we can be more refreshed by going to a good party than we would have been by sitting home and feeling tired. And the purpose of the changes in the liturgy is to make Sunday Mass a real celebration, a sacred recreation.

So this problem comes down to that of changing our expectations of what we are meant to "get out of" going to Mass — the rest and refreshment that comes from action, rather than from inaction; from interest rather than passivity; from sharing in a community enterprise rather than from relaxing by oneself. Christ indeed told us that he came to give us peace, but he did not mean the peace of vegetables: "I am come that they may live, and live more intensely." This is what the "new" Mass is all about.

Mysteriousness versus Mystery

When I was child, I used to get a kind of holy thrill out of going, on a bright afternoon, into our enormous old parish church — the darkness, broken here and there by twinkling vigil lights and colors from the stained-glass windows; the white high altar that soared in tiers of statues and marble curlicues up into the dimness of the roof; the faint smell of incense; the organist softly practicing up in the choir loft. And, at Sunday Mass, I enjoyed seeing the altar all illuminated and watching (my mother always marched us well up in front) what went on in the sanctuary and hearing something of what the poet Browning called "the blessed mutter of the Mass." All this meant "holiness" to me, and I loved it and was comforted by it — as innumerable Catholics have loved and been comforted by a similar atmosphere in their churches and their worship.

But now, it seems, the Church is trying to do away with a great many of these things that religion has meant to a vast number of her members. A "dim religious light" is out; new churches are generally much brighter as well as much barer than the old ones. And the "blessed mutter" is on its way out everywhere. The priest is speaking aloud and directly to us, and — at least some of the time — in our own language; where he needs a loudspeaker to be heard by everyone, he is using one. When the priest does lapse into Latin, it doesn't seem particularly sacred any more, but only a confusing foreign intervention — and even the most ardent anti-vernacularist can hardly help hoping that now that the Church has gone this far, she will go all the way and allow the whole Mass to be in the language of the people. And we hear that more revisions are being worked out to make the sacred rites still clearer and more understandable.

But, many people wonder, is the Catholic religion meant to be such an out-in-the-open, understandable affair? Isn't there any value in the sense of mystery, of awe in the presence of the sacred, that was nourished by the dim churches, the Latin, the incomprehensible rites of the past? Will we Catholics continue to be religious-minded now that we are doing away with the character-istically "mysterious" atmosphere once proper to the Roman Catholic religion?

The answer is that this kind of a sense of mystery has very little to do with Christianity. St. Paul often speaks about "the mystery of Christ." But he doesn't mean either "mysteriousness" or "mystery" in the sense of a "mystery story." He means, on the contrary, God's *revelation* to men of his plan for our salvation, the plan that had been hidden in his wisdom through the ages and was finally revealed and realized in Christ. This mystery is now revealed to us in the Church, where we come also to share in it. And this is done above all in the celebration of the eucharist, where we do not *do* it in a cloud of incense or nonsense, but rather "*proclaim* the death of the Lord until he comes."

In Christianity, then, our sense of awe, of prostrate adoration, of unworthiness in the presence of the Holy, is meant to be nourished, not by *not* hearing and seeing and understanding the visible signs of Christ's presence and action — the sacramental words and rites — but rather *by* seeing, hearing, taking part and trying to understand in order to believe more fully, and so entering all our lives more and more deeply into "the unsearchable riches of Christ."

We need not regret the vanishing of the religious atmosphere of our childhood. There are better things ahead if, with and in the Church, we try to open our minds and hearts to the *light* of Christ.

But Latin
Is So Beautiful!

A student was commenting recently on the "new liturgy" as celebrated in the monastic church of his college. "You know," he said, "the monks used to sing a high Mass on Sundays with Gregorian chant and all that. Now they have one of those Masses with English hymns instead, and they all sing those. The words aren't much good and the tunes don't seem anything great either. It seems kind of too bad."

If the younger generation feel that something has been lost, as we move into a new age of Catholic worship, how much more does the old — especially those of us who studied Latin and who sang in choirs and knew the real joy of Gregorian chant from within. The Latin of the liturgy, well said or sung, is beautiful — most of it, anyway. Gregorian chant properly carried out can indeed seem like the singing of the heavenly choirs. Must we lose all this beauty and accept instead the flat and jerky English of a great part of the present translations, the uninspiring words and music of many of the hymns now being sung at Mass?

It seems as though we must if we are to go forward toward forms of Catholic worship that are beautiful and *living*. Latin is not a living language for American Catholics. Gregorian chant is not a living musical language. The Latin liturgy and the treasures of Gregorian chant have become museum pieces. We may appreciate them and love them — but they cannot serve the needs of the Christian life today.

Our ancestors who came to this country had, in many cases, to leave many values behind them in order to create a new life in a new country. So Catholics today have to leave behind much that is truly valuable, as well as much that is not, in order to live the Christian life in today's world, not in yesterday's, as the Church is asking them to do. We can't live in a museum anymore, even if what is in it is more beautiful than what is — as yet — outside. And the fact is that the Church faces such vast problems today in trying to reexpress her message and live her life in modern terms because Catholics have been too museum-minded during the last few centuries.

But this does not mean that we ought to reconcile ourselves to the poor English and the second-rate music that characterize far too much of the present liturgy. Modern American English can be noble and clear and powerful. In the vast treasury of Christian hymns, many can be found that people today could really sing from their hearts if noble modern words were fitted to the noble melodies. And modern poets and composers exist who — if they were encouraged — could create hymns which would be authentic expressions, in today's musical and verbal idiom, of Christian joy and sorrow, praise and petition.

Our job today is not to cling to or regret the

vanishing of old modes of expression. It is to do whatever we can to encourage and create the new ones that Christian worship and Christian life need today. All of us can pray, and pray earnestly, that the Holy Spirit may guide and inspire all those who are responsible for the language and music of the liturgy. And we can also pray that he may open our own minds and hearts to welcome good new forms of expression whenever and from wherever they may come. For to live in the present and to be ready to embrace the future is always the Christian attitude. As St. Paul says, "Forgetting what lies behind and straining forward to what lies ahead, I press on toward the goal for the prize of the upward call of God in Christ Jesus."

Can't I Use
My Missal Anymore?

When I was in college in New York, my brother — who was a music critic — used to take me with him to the opera. He would provide me beforehand with a libretto, giving a synopsis of the plot, notes about the composer and so on, and the whole text in English. I soon found that it was rather hopeless to try to follow the arias and choruses word by word. The best thing to do was to read the introductory material and the text ahead of time, and then just look and listen.

Of course I was just a member of the audience. The singers themselves had spent months and even years in studying that libretto, in analyzing the music and the words, in equipping themselves with the knowledge and technique to interpret and express it according to the intentions of the composer. One can't imagine an opera singer going through a real performance with a libretto in hand, or an actor on opening night clinging to the text of the play. Both singers and actors have studied their parts and studied the whole play and a great many other things *before* they take part in a performance.

The same is true about the use of a missal. It provides the text or libretto for a given Mass. A good modern missal also gives a great deal of valuable information about the structure of the Mass, the season or the feast, and about each text. Such a missal is an invaluable tool for intelligent participation in the Mass. But, even if we were only part of the "audience" at a Mass, we should be looking and listening, not reading all the time. And since we are participators, clearly we should not have our noses buried in a book. The time to use a missal is not *at* Mass, but in preparing for Mass.

True, we needed missals at Mass when the changing parts were all in Latin and when, in many churches, we couldn't hear what was being said anyway. But with a properly celebrated "modern" Mass, you should not need a missal except when you are in such a foggy state that you really need to read the text of the canon to keep your mind from wandering. (We should all pray that *soon* the whole Mass will be in worthy English, and the canon said *aloud,* and then we won't need missals at Mass at all.)

But this does not mean that the age of the missal is over. It should just be beginning. The *Constitution on the Sacred Liturgy* stresses again and again the need for "liturgical education," and no better tool exists for our own self-education than one of the good modern missals. And there is no better tool for use in family preparation for Sunday Mass, and for discussion clubs and classes.

Such missals are useful also in another way. We receive the bread of God's Word as well as the bread of the eucharist at Sunday Mass, and at every Mass. We need to take time to digest it and assimilate it by reading it over and thinking it over and making it truly our own — this is the original form of Christian "mental prayer." And for this we need both a bible and a missal.

So, if you own a good missal and have put it away on a shelf, go and dust it off and begin to put it to its proper use. And if you don't own one, go and buy one. We can't expect priests to give us all the liturgical education we need to make our participation in the Mass what it should be — let alone to make it fully fruitful in our lives. We are, certainly, to stop being "missal-bound" at Mass. But if we can read, we need to become properly missal-minded as an aid to help us "have that mind which was in Christ Jesus."

II
COMING TOGETHER AND
HEARING THE WORD OF GOD

Starting Out
Right

An eminent Catholic speaker and writer remarked to me several years ago that he had heard that "those liturgists" wanted to get rid of the prayers at the foot of the altar. He hoped that they never would succeed, he said, because it's so healthy for priests and lay people to be admitting that they are sinners, publicly and at the same time. Now what he feared is happening — congregations are asked to sing a hymn while the priest and servers are saying these prayers, which have already been shortened and, probably, in the revised liturgy, will become what they once were, part of the priest's private preparation. A great many people miss them — if not for the reason given above, at least because these prayers seemed a good way to ease into the Mass, to go from the distractions of ordinary life to the altar of God.

The fact is that these prayers at the foot of the altar aren't suitable for the first act of a Mass that is going to be a real celebration. It would be rather odd — in our culture anyway — if the first thing you were expected to do when you went to a party was to explain how unworthy you felt to be there. You say, rather, to your host or hostess how *glad* you are to be there. And, after that, the first thing that happens at a party or celebration is some kind of mutual greeting and introducing, so that all the people present begin to form a real gathering, a community, ready for whatever is to be done.

So it is at Mass. We are asked to join in singing a hymn to start off with, so as to express to God our gladness at having come together to take part in the eucharist. We join in saying the introit verses which set the keynote for the celebration. Then we greet him who has gathered us together, who is present among us because we are together in his name. We call him by his great titles, "Lord" and "Christ," asking his mercy because he is our God and savior. When the "Glory to God in the highest" follows, it gives us the opportunity to express still further our gladness, our appreciation and our praise — to the Father whose love has brought us all here into his presence, and to the Son with whom we dare to come into that presence in the Spirit. And, finally, the priest invites us to pray, and then voices our prayer in the collect, offering it to the Father through Christ.

So the Mass begins. This is the "entrance rite," the sacred equivalent of the greeting and introducing that takes place at the beginning of an ordinary human celebration. It helps us to realize that we all have come together to form a community with the celebrant and his ministers and with Christ our Lord, a community coming together into the presence of the Father. Now we are ready to hear God's Word together and to celebrate the eucharist.

Isn't this really better than the way Mass used to

begin, with all of us just settling down quietly to try to follow the priest from our missals or to say our own prayers? Isn't it more Christian?

But what about the need to have some transition from our usual thoughts and preoccupations to get us ready for Mass? In one sense, we shouldn't need any. Sunday Mass — and daily Mass, when we can get to it — is meant to be the heart, the focus *of* our lives, not something apart, cut off from them. Our whole week should lead from and to the Mass, should be a follow-up of one Sunday's Mass and the preparation for the next. It is a good idea, too, to prepare for Mass by studying and thinking about it the night before, and also by getting there a few minutes ahead of time and praying along the lines of the present prayers at the foot of the altar. But then, when the Mass begins, join in and begin the celebration with all your fellow-guests.

Don't You Think
He Can Read?

I had an actor friend once who had played in a series of Shakespearian plays in a midwestern city. He said that one of the most unnerving experiences of the season occurred one day when he was playing Jacques in *As You Like It* and was being distracted by the loud rustling of turning pages all through the audience. When he could take a good look, he discovered that it was composed mainly of ladies, and he thought they must be teachers because each was armed with her own copy of Shakespeare from which she was busily following the play. He managed to distract them from their books, however, when he got to "All the world's a stage . . ." because he knew that these lines were written in gold all around the proscenium arch of the theatre. So he came out and paused long enough to get attention, and then very deliberately turned around and read from the lettering. He got a laugh — and less page-turning.

Every Sunday at Mass, I am reminded of this incident and wish the priest could think of some similar way to cope with the situation. Every pew is provided with leaflet missals, in case you want to follow the Latin parts or forget the new wording of the creed. But many of my fellow parishioners are reading and turning pages while the lector is reading the epistle, and while the celebrant is reading the gradual and the Gospel. Are they hard of hearing or are the acoustics poor? Or do they want to check on the differences between the translations in the altar missal and the leaflet missal? This is an interesting occupation, but surely not for Mass. Or don't they think that the lector and the celebrant can read? (This idea annoys me because my husband is the lector at our Mass, and he reads very well.)

Why are so many people wedded to reading at Mass when they should be listening? Some say the trouble is that our whole culture is eye-minded rather than ear-minded. Others say that very few people are used to hearing someone else read aloud. It seems strange to be just sitting, or standing, and listening when they could be reading to themselves. (Equally, of course, few people read aloud *well*. They don't make it easy to listen and understand. This is certainly a problem which seminaries, and pastors who have to train lectors, need to take very seriously if we are going to be able really to hear the Word of God when we do listen.)

But the basic difficulty lies deeper, I think. A great many Catholics aren't yet really convinced of the fact that the Mass is a dialogue, a sacred conversation, as well as an action, between God and his people. During a great part of the Mass, we are speaking to God our Father, aware that we are doing so with Christ. Sometimes we all speak or sing together; sometimes the priest speaks for us. But we are always speaking *to* someone. And in the epistle and Gospel, God speaks *to us* through the human voice of Christ's minister as he reads us the inspired words of holy scripture. That human voice, speaking those inspired words, is a "sacrament" — in the wide sense of a "sacred sign" — of Christ the incarnate Word of the Father, giving us the Father's message of love.

Now, you don't read your part in a conversation; you speak it. And you don't read, if you are at all polite, while someone is speaking to you; you listen. And besides, there is a profound difference between reading separately and *listening together*. People who could have stayed home and read the president's inaugural address went to a vast amount of trouble to go to Washington and hear him speak it, and millions of us who couldn't go listened to it over TV and radio rather than reading it later. We wanted to hear *him,* and we wanted to hear him *together* as fellow Americans listening to our president addressing us each and all on matters of importance.

How much more, then, should we put away our missals at Mass and listen to Christ who, as the *Constitution on the Sacred Liturgy* says, "is present in his Word, since it is he himself who speaks when the holy scriptures are read in the Church"?

Are You Afraid
of the Bible?

Just after World War II, my husband helped to tutor a young man of French-Canadian background who had lost almost all his sight in the service. He went home one weekend proudly carrying a braille bible given him by the priest who had introduced him to us. His mother was deeply shocked. "You couldn't have got that from a priest," she said. "You know Catholics aren't allowed to read the bible."

Most of us wouldn't have put it so strongly, even fifteen or twenty years ago. After all, salesmen representing Catholic firms have been going around selling bibles for a long time with full ecclesiastical approval. And anyone who looked inside could see that an indulgence was granted for reading the holy book fifteen minutes a day. But somehow the great majority of adult Catholics grew up with the idea that the bible was rather a dangerous book to try to read. Doesn't the Church say that one mustn't read it except in a Catholic version and with notes? And, anyhow, why read it? Surely the Church gives us all the truths we need for salvation in the catechism, neatly and accurately expressed. So why

41

risk some danger to one's faith by trying to find them in the bible? After all, that's what the Protestants did.

Ideas like this, floating round in the back of our minds, are a great obstacle to our cooperating with the Church's present effort to "promote that warm and living love for scripture to which the venerable tradition of both Eastern and Western rites gives testimony" (*Constitution on the Sacred Liturgy,* n. 24). Why all of a sudden is the Church making such a big deal about the "liturgy of the Word" — what we used to call the "Mass of the catechumens" and think of as a kind of soothing and non-essential preliminary (after all, you didn't have to be on time for it)? And why bible services? Weren't the old devotions good enough?

The answer is that the Church is calling on us to grow up. Children accept their parents as part of the scheme of things; they run to them when they are hurt or need something. But they aren't capable of really entering into their parents' plans and hopes, of being their friends. Too many of us have been thus childish in our relations with God our Father and with our Lord, the incarnate *Word* of the Father. The Church wants us to begin to realize that he wants to make us his friends, and so he wants to speak to us — not just in formulas, but in living words about events and persons and ideas. And he does so in the Church, above all in the liturgy and in holy scripture. "It is he himself who speaks when the holy scriptures are read in the Church" (*Constitution on the Sacred Liturgy,* n. 7).

The point here, of course, is "read in the Church." We are not to be left alone with a book to find Christ. We are to hear him "in the Church," sharing in the Church's understanding of what he is saying to all of us as a community and to each of us as persons in that community. And the place we do this, above all, is when we listen to the epistle and Gospel of the Mass, in the context of the Mass, with the words of Christ's minister in the sermon to help us understand more fully. Bible services, in the same way, allow Christ to speak to us through scripture in the context of the understanding and praying Church. And our private praying and studying of the bible, in the same way, is always to be done "in the Church." This is why her scholars and pastors are pouring out books and pamphlets to help us hear Christ, the Word of God, in the inspired words, and not just our own or somebody else's ideas.

May we, then, put away our distrust of holy scripture and begin to welcome it — in the Mass and in bible services and as part of our prayer-life — as the "bread of the Word," given us to help us "grow up in all things in Christ."

"He Who Has Ears . . . ."

Every parent has noted the odd fact that his children can be quite deaf to shouts of "Stop that!" and similar admonitions, though they are quite able to hear even whispered parental discussions that they think might concern them. Of course, grown-ups are like this too. Even if our ears are in excellent condition, we can be psychologically deaf. How often, for instance, do husbands complain, "You never told me anything about that," when reminded that they have to go out to some affair that they don't expect to enjoy.

Many Catholics come to Mass afflicted with this psychological deafness. In his parable about the farmer who went out to sow his seed, our Lord tells us some of the things which keep people from holding on to and making good use of what he has to say. But too many of us don't really hear him at all. We come to Mass prepared *not* to listen to the Word of God because we don't expect it to have any real interest for us.

Of course, all during our lives we have been de-conditioned for real listening to the scripture readings at Mass. After all, one didn't really need to hear the priest or see the altar in order to fulfill one's Sunday obliga-

tion. Besides, the official reading of the epistle and
Gospel was apparently intended to be heard by God
alone, since it was done in Latin and facing the altar.

Now these obvious difficulties are being remedied.
The readings are carried out in our own language, and
the reader faces us. Most churches that need them are
being equipped with loudspeakers, and altars are being
placed where everyone can see them. It is clear that the
Church really wants us to *hear*.

But many of us still come to Mass more or less
psychologically deaf. This is due in part, probably, to
the vague distrust of scripture just discussed. But it is
also caused by the fact that we are not used to thinking
of holy scripture as *communication,* as God's way of
telling us things that could be of intense interest to us if
we really listened to them. We think of the bible as
containing many edifying stories and parables. Perhaps
we remember bits of a course in "bible history." But
nothing we know about the bible makes it seem like
"the *Word* of God" — the Word he wants us to hear.

And so, it is a new idea, and one that we find hard
to take in, not only that it is Christ himself who "speaks
when the holy scriptures are read in the Church," but
also that he is actually saying things to us, here and
now, that he wants us to hear and think about and
respond to.

One trouble is, of course, that we have heard the
same epistles and Gospels and read them in our missals
for years and years. How can they be *new* communica-
tions? The Church is going to help us here, so far as
normal boredom is concerned, by giving us a two- or
three-year cycle of readings when the rites are revised,
so that we shall hear more of scripture in the Sunday
Masses and hear the same passage less frequently.

But the real point is that, while scripture remains the same, it is always the living Christ who speaks through a passage to *us,* the persons and community to whom it is read this Sunday. Since the last time we heard this epistle or Gospel, we have changed and so has the whole world; we have all moved forward in history, nearer to the Lord's return in glory. Christ is speaking to us as we are *now,* and giving us his Spirit to help us find new aspects of the infinite wealth of meaning *for us* that he wants to communicate to us. If we try to hear him speaking, and speaking to us, we shall begin to find this meaning.

Knowing and
Knowing About

Near the end of Dorothy Sayers' classic detective novel, *Gaudy Night,* she describes the hero and heroine going to a concert together, and she gives the heroine's meditations on the different ways in which the people around them were listening to the music, a Bach fugue. There were those who just pretended to like music but were really thinking about something else altogether; and the people, like herself, who enjoyed the music and could follow it in a kind of way; and the rare listeners, like her escort, who could really hear the interweaving melodies without effort, so that they could fully listen with heart and mind at once.

We Catholics, equally, vary in our ability to really hear the Word of God when it is read to us in the Mass, or at a bible service, or when we read it ourselves. And too few of us are in the skilled category; we have never really found out what to listen for. But it is vital to the renewal that we really try to hear what God wants to tell us in his holy Word. For it is very difficult to be interested in him and in what he asks of us unless we are continually coming to know him better.

Now there is one very important kind of listening that we are often hardly aware of when we do it — listening to the person behind the words. In any real conversation, especially with someone we want to know well, we try to find out more about *him* from what he is saying, as well as to hear what he has to say. People who make important business deals by telephone with persons they have never met personally get great skill in judging someone's character and personality from his voice over the phone, from the way he expresses himself and organizes his ideas, making an effort to reach out and contact the person behind the voice. And anyone who is in love has the "ears of his heart" as well as his physical ears wide open to come to know the beloved person better, even when they are talking about the weather.

And, of course, people who want to know one another better make a positive effort to open themselves out, to let themselves be really known by one another. They not only tell one another *about* themselves; they try to meet one another as persons through the medium of speech.

So it is with God's inspired Word and with the whole liturgy. Through human words about events and people and their actions and reactions, and through the persons and acts as well as the words of the liturgy, God wants to make *himself* known to us. He wants us to know him as our Father who desires really to speak, to communicate with us through his Son, his incarnate Word, so that we may know him as his own Son knows him.

When we listen to the epistle and Gospel at Mass, we might then first ask ourselves what God is telling us about himself, not only in so many words, like "God is love," but in what the sacred text reveals about his ways of acting, his ways of expressing himself in human language.

When we read the Gospel, for instance, everything that our Lord does as well as everything he says reveals his personality, to use our modern term. As St. Augustine says, "All the deeds of the Word are words to us." And we know that our Lord told Philip at the Last Supper, "He who sees me, sees the Father also."

May we practice listening, then, not only to the words, but to the Person behind the words, and ask the Holy Spirit given us at our baptism to help us truly hear the voice of God today.

A Sour Note
on Translations

A correspondent writes: "You say that in the epistle and Gospel God speaks to us through the human voice of Christ's minister as he reads the inspired words of holy scripture. This is the way I used to feel — but the 'new' scripture translation doesn't sound 'holy' and not even 'pleasing' — in fact, it is offensive, common, trite and juvenile. It just isn't possible to imagine God telling us to 'fasten our belts,' and 'Get up, girl' sounds like 'Giddy up, horsie'. . . . I am not an intellectual; I do not claim to be theologian. But ignorant as I am, I loved the musical cadence of the old translation where Christ spoke to the soul and the soul answered Christ."

This letter brings up a problem which I am as troubled by as is my correspondent. I have been avoiding it up to this point both because it is a very complex one and because I don't enjoy criticizing the hard-working scholars who did their best, under great pressure, to produce the present translations of the epistles and Gospels. But if these translations are an obstacle to hearing God's Word to people like my correspondent as well as to people who might call themselves intellectuals, then this problem should be discussed.

First, it should be said that if you have been really familiar with one of the old translations of scripture from your earliest years, if you have meditated on cherished phrases and let them resound in your mind in times of stress and of joy, if they are a part of you — then you aren't going to welcome *any* new translation easily. (In St. Jerome's time, when the "common people" really knew scripture, there was a real fuss at his changing, in his new translation, even the kind of bush that Jonah sat under.) But there is a real need in the Church for new translations whenever existing ones become archaic. God's Word needs to be rendered in language that makes it seem of urgent and immediate import to each generation, "as sharp as a two-edged sword" — and it doesn't seem so to most people today when it is in 17th-century English, however beautiful. So we older people must be openminded about new translations, even though we, personally, are quite happy with the old ones.

But it is sad indeed that, just when the Church is calling us to a "warm and living love for holy scripture," we should be given what we are being given. The scholars who produced the current translations know the ancient language; they are experts on the "literary forms" of scripture. But because of the defects of our educational system and general lack of culture, they don't really know English, with its wonderful variety of resources, its different levels of "colloquiality," its many possibilities of spoken cadence. (As a friend of mine said of the Confraternity version of the psalms, "It's like riding in a car with broken springs.")

The scholars who produced the present readings

for the Mass were trying to render faithfully the original in clear, simple English. But they have never had the opportunity to acquire the "ear" for spoken and written English needed to achieve their aim. A scholar in the 1920s, Rev. C. F. Burney, wrote a book called "The Poetry of our Lord," showing how his discourses, as set down in the Gospels, are cast in the forms of Hebrew poetry. You would certainly never suspect anything of the kind from the present Gospel readings. It is hard to see how the crowds could have cried out in admiration that no man had ever spoken like this man, if he had used the inept, semi-colloquial, semi-pedantic style characterizing so many of the readings we are now hearing at Mass.

We shall just have to be patient, pray that better things will come when the rites are revised, and try to hear the Lord speaking to us through the very distracting static of these translations.

"That Red Sea Stuff"

A priest friend of ours told us that back in 1957, the year after the first introduction of the revised Holy Week rites, the bishop of his diocese sent out directives to pastors reminding them that they must take pains again that year to prepare their people to take part in the Holy Week services and outlining some sermons for this purpose. Our friend dropped into a pastor's study as he was opening his letter from the bishop. He scanned the pages and groaned, "Do I have to go into that Red Sea stuff again this year?"

Many Catholics, like this good pastor, have wondered about the "Red Sea stuff" and all the other Old Testament selections and allusions that they found in their missals, particularly during Lent and Holy Week. And the many Lenten daily Mass-goers who never used missals will be wondering too, now that they hear the readings in English. The art of Christian listening to the Word of God, an art so highly cultivated in the early centuries of the Church, has been almost lost for quite a while and we are only beginning to regain it. What is God telling us about himself and ourselves in these Old Testament accounts of wonders and miracles,

53

punishments and rescues — or in the accounts of our Lord's own miracles, for that matter? We know the stories; we heard them all in bible history courses in childhood. Why should we hear them again and again each year?

As has already been suggested, we will not find any scripture selection dull if we really try to listen to the Person behind the words, to the incarnate Word of the Father speaking to us here and now. But we may still ask: Why is he telling us, for instance, about Elias bringing the son of a widowed woman to life, or about the misdeeds of the Israelites of old and how he urged them to repentance? What message have these passages for us?

If you take the two readings of many of the Lenten Masses together, the answer suggests itself. For instance, the story about Elias bringing the son of the widow back to life is followed by St. John's account of our Lord bringing Lazarus back to life. And these passages are read to us in *Lent,* the time of penance and preparation for the renewal of the grace of our baptism. Through both these "wonderful works" of God's mercy, then, he is telling us that he can and will bring *us* back to life. He is describing, in terms of these two physical miracles of the past, what he does for people today through the Church, most particularly by the sacraments of baptism and penance. How more vividly could he make us realize, and realize afresh each year, that these sacraments are really *life*-giving?

Or again, in another Lenten Mass there are three readings — two from the Old Testament giving God's promises to "pour clean water" upon his people, to cleanse them of their sins if they will repent and "come to the aid of the oppressed," and the third giving the

Gospel account of our Lord curing the man born blind by putting clay on his eyes and sending him to wash in the pool of Siloe. In the context of Lent, with the Easter Vigil drawing near, these readings are meant to make us realize that baptism is at once cleansing and enlightening. The newly-baptized can say with the man born blind, "Now I see!" One of the names for baptism in the early Church was "illumination." And when we renew the grace of our baptism at the Easter Vigil, we should see *better* — know God better and see everything more clearly in the light of his love.

Through holy scripture, then, God shows us the outlines, the design, the shape of his dealings with *us,* in terms of his dealings with other people. As Fr. Louis Bouyer puts it, scripture gives us the inspired account of "the common experience of God and mankind." And so it lights up our own experience of him in the Church and shows us how to understand and enter into it more fully. That "Red Sea stuff" really isn't so stuffy after all!

About Sermons

I once met a lady who was concerned with the promotion of an organization that called itself, if I remember rightly, *The Association for the Improvement of Preaching*. She said that she had never yet met a priest who declined to join.

The *Constitution on the Sacred Liturgy* says this about sermons: "Because the sermon is part of the liturgical service, the best place for it is to be indicated even in the rubrics, as far as the nature of the rite will allow; the ministry of preaching is to be fulfilled with exactitude and fidelity. The sermon, moreover, should draw its content mainly from scriptural and liturgical sources, and its character should be that of a proclamation of God's wonderful works in the history of salvation, the mystery of Christ, ever made present and active within us, especially in the liturgy."

And again, in connection with the Mass, the Constitution says: "By means of the homily, the mysteries of the faith and the guiding principles of the Christian life are expounded from the sacred text during the course of the liturgical year; the homily, therefore, is to be highly esteemed *as a part of the liturgy itself*" (italics mine). And so, the experts tell us, in the traditional thinking of the Church, God is speaking to us, not only in the epistle and the Gospel, but also in the sermon or homily. Here the accredited minister of Christ and the Church should open out to us the meaning of the sacred texts as they apply to our special needs.

This is what a sermon ought to be and do. But many of us have heard many sermons that didn't try to do this, as well as many that tried but didn't succeed. After all, our priests were not trained to give sermons of this sort, but rather — if any real training was afforded them in the seminary — to give doctrinal instructions or exhortations, or, what the Italians call so well, *fervorinos*. But now that the place of the sermon in the Mass, its function and its nature have been unmistakably indicated by the Constitution, and now that the education in seminaries is to be centered in the mystery of Christ and the history of salvation in such a way as to make clear the connection of the sacred sciences with the liturgy, things ought to improve wherever improvement is needed.

In the meantime we ourselves can do something to help bring about this improvement. Anyone who has ever given a public talk realizes how much difference the attentiveness and interest of the audience can make in the quality of one's talk. A "dead" audience can defeat the most skillful and inspired of speakers. Glance about you at next Sunday's Mass. Observe how many of the congregation look as if they had any hope of hearing anything of interest. How would you like to address such an audience?

Would it not help our priests, then, in their efforts to give better sermons every Sunday in accordance with the spirit and the directives of the Constitution, if we laity made an effort to pay at least reasonably polite attention to them? It would be worth trying, anyway — especially for those of us who are inclined to be critical or who are used to thinking of this period as one for relaxation or for mulling over personal problems.

An old nun once told me, in speaking of all the sermons she had listened to and of their general mediocrity: "But I always find that if I really try to listen, the Lord has something to say to me in every sermon — something I really need to hear." Maybe if we all tried to listen in the same spirit, we would find this true for us also.

"Ask and You Shall Receive . . . ."

Fr. Gerald Ellard, S.J., of blessed memory, once told us that, while waiting for a friend to come out of church, he heard one lady say to another, "Well, I've got four novenas going and one of them ought to hit the jackpot!" As Louis Everly points out in his book, *We Dare To Say Our Father,* few of us really do treat God as a Father. Surely, the kind of "devotion" represented by the lady who made the remark just quoted treats God as a kind of divine roulette wheel.

But the common Catholic practice of "saying five *Our Father's* and five *Hail Mary's*" for this or that intention does not treat God as a Father either. The *Our Father* is the "Lord's Prayer," to be said meaningfully with Christ. It is meant to be the model for all our praying — "This is how you should pray . . ." — but not to be repeated until it becomes meaningless. It would certainly be a very odd family indeed in which, when a child wanted money to go to the movies, he was expected to come up to his father and recite a formula five times "for the intention" of being given movie money. Why don't we come right out and ask God for what we need?

The reintroduction of the "prayer of the faithful" in the Mass, at the conclusion of the service of the Word, is meant to bring us back to this simple, direct, personal approach to the Father in heaven, which is the essence of Christian prayer. In it we ask God for the needs of the Church and of human society, of our parish community and of individuals. It offers scope for presenting specific needs to our Father's notice as well as individual ones, and for varying them in accordance with circumstances. And since we are praying for what we want *together,* our asking has the assurance of Christ's promise: "If two of you shall agree on earth about anything at all for which they ask, it shall be done for them by my Father in heaven. For where two or three are gathered together for my sake, there am I in the midst of you."

This "prayer of the faithful" is nothing new in the Roman liturgy; it remained in the Good Friday services all through the centuries (and a remnant of it also in the prayers asked for the faithful departed and the sick of a parish after the announcements at a Mass and before the Gospel). Its reintroduction, in a litany form which allows for variety and adaptation to what is going on in the Church and the world and our parish, shows us the Church's concern that we bring our lives and our needs and our interests with us to Mass, that we do not come just as "souls," but as whole human persons, to worship our Father with Christ in spirit and in truth. It shows her concern that we realize afresh the fact that our religion is a person-to-Person affair, not a station-to-station one, and that we are not less ourselves, but more so, when we pray together. Christian community prayer is not meant to be impersonal, any more than individual prayer is.

We may hope, then, that besides the general petitions for the needs of the Church and the world, priests will increasingly include specific needs suggested by what is happening in the world and in each parish and to individual families and persons within a parish. We need all the help we can get to realize that God is our Father, concerned about all our needs, and that since he is *our* Father, we must be concerned about one another's needs in the love of Christ.

A Question of
When and How

Most parents find, sooner or later, that the only way to make possible anything like an orderly conversation at meals is to leave a reasonable space of time at the beginning for all the requests like "Butter, please!" "May I get the ketchup?" "I need a quarter for the scout meeting." If this isn't done, the conversation will be interrupted because such requests have to be made sooner or later.

Experts say that a similar need may account for the interruption of the canon of the Mass — essentially a prayer of praise and thanksgiving — by the mementos of the living and the dead. There wasn't enough scope given to prayers of petition for individuals elsewhere in the Mass, so they were put in where they don't really belong. In any case, the reintroduction of the "prayer of the faithful" at the end of the service of the Word now gives the voicing of our concrete needs its proper scope in the Mass, and so may help also to give it its proper place in all our prayer and in all our lives.

By taking part in this "prayer of the faithful," we pray together for the Church, the pope, our bishop, our priests and all our brothers and sisters in Christ, for human society and its needs, and for individuals. And we do so as part of our response to God's Word just given to us in the epistle and Gospel and sermon. We have just told God, in the words of the creed, that we believe in him, our Father, in his Son and in the Spirit; we believe everything that he has told us, everything that he has done, is doing and will do to bring us all to share his life in love. And now we ask him for the blessings that the Church and the world and individual people need in order to cooperate with his work.

This including of "asking" prayers in our response to God's Word is based on the very nature and structure of Christian prayer (as Fr. Louis Bouyer, for example, points out in his *Introduction to Spirituality*). In truly Christian prayer, we do not ask God to do *our* will; we ask for the means to do *his* will. And so, all Christian prayer in one way or another begins with *listening* to God and goes on to welcome what we have heard and to ask him to enable us to carry it out.

This is why the classic collect prayers, at the end of the entrance rite of the Mass, usually have the pattern: "O God, who . . . grant us that. . . ." For it is on the basis of what God has done for us in sacred history, revealed to us by his Word, that we ask him to go on acting along the same lines, so to speak, and to carry on and complete his work in us by giving us the blessings we need. And, in the service of the Word, we hear the epistle and Gospel and sermon, and then respond with the creed and with our petitions.

The "prayer of petition," therefore, isn't an inferior form of prayer for people with their minds too much on their own needs to concentrate on praise and thanksgiving. It has its proper place in every Christian's prayer as it has in the Mass. The point is whether we do it in the spirit of "gimme!" or of "I've said so many prayers or made this or that sacrifice and so you owe me this favor," or whether we try to ask for what we need as a response to God's love, a form of praise of his goodness, an answer to his call. As St. Paul says, "Have no anxiety, but in every prayer and supplication with thanksgiving let your petitions be made known to God." This is what the "prayer of the faithful" now enables us to do better, and to do together, at Mass.

III
THE BREAD AND WINE
ON THE ALTAR AND THE "OFFERTORY"

Getting
Ready

Most parents agree that the time just before dinner is the most difficult period of the day. Basically the problem is a simple one — to get the people around the table and the food on it so that everything is ready for saying grace and sitting down to eat. But whatever one does ahead of time, there always seems to be some confusion. Someone hasn't washed his hands and has to be sent off to do so while the rest wait. Two other members of the family are involved in a conversation and can't be torn away from it. There are too many helpers or too few to put the food in an orderly way on the table. It is hard to find an ideal solution for all circumstances.

The history of what we now call the "offertory" of the Mass shows that the Church has had somewhat similar difficulties through the centuries with the immediate preparations for the eucharistic meal. As long as the celebration of the eucharist was joined to a regular meal, as at the Last Supper, there was no problem: bread and wine were already on the table. And when the eucharist began to be celebrated quite apart from

an ordinary meal, bread and wine and water at first
were simply brought in with no ceremony and put on
the table.

Later on, in line with an emphasis on the value of
material creation against heretics who denied it, the
bread and wine to be used for the eucharist came more
clearly to be seen as offerings taken from material
creation, symbolizing the Christians' self-offering to
God to be taken up into the current of Christ's self-
offering. It became customary for Christians to bring
bread and wine, together with their gifts for the needs
of the Church and the poor, whenever they came to take
part in the eucharist, and various methods were developed of presenting these offerings and conveying the
bread and wine for the eucharist to the altar.

In Africa, for instance, in St. Augustine's time, the
people brought their offerings up to the altar; the
priest received them and then set apart what was
needed for the eucharist. In 7th-century Rome, the
celebrant and his assistants went around and collected
bread and wine from the people. (This is the origin of
the ceremony of the "lavabo" — the celebrant needed
to wash his hands which had become sticky in handling
loaves and jugs of wine.) So the offertory chant, of
which our present offertory verse is a token, was developed to accompany the procession with the gifts, as
the prayer over the gifts expresses the offering of the
gifts and ourselves to God. In other places the people
brought their gifts to a special side room when they
first came to church, and what was to be used for the
eucharist was brought up and placed on the altar at
the beginning of the eucharistic part of the service.
This "great entrance" is a very prominent part of the
present Byzantine liturgy, for instance.

So far, what was done was still clearly in the framework of preparation for the sacrifice-banquet. But then things began to get confused. In our Roman rite, the people no longer brought bread and wine as offerings, but money instead (which is why the collection is taken up at this point in the Mass). And the celebrant began to engage in a private conversation, as it were, with God, describing and offering the bread and wine as if they had already become Christ's body and blood. But he continued to wash his hands, although this was no longer needed. And this action was given, by the psalm that accompanies it, the meaning of a desire for spiritual cleanness in order to take part worthily in Christ's sacrifice — a desire already expressed in one way or another in the prayer over the gifts.

The present prayers and actions carried out by the priest between the offertory verse and the prayer over the gifts are, therefore, rather like the various distractions that can delay beginning a family meal. The essence of this part of the Mass, and what we need to concentrate on during it, is the presentation of ourselves and our gifts to God in the spirit indicated by the offertory antiphon and the prayer over the gifts. Surely this is enough!

Our
Contribution

Every mother of a large family knows how pleasant it is when guests coming for dinner bring some contributions to the meal — a cake, some rolls, a bottle of wine. Not only are the gifts themselves welcome, but even more the intention that prompted them — the guests' desire to contribute to the pleasure of the occasion, to share what they have with their hosts as their hosts are sharing with them.

But it would be very embarrassing if, instead of simply saying something like, "I'm so glad to be with you. Here is something I hope you can use," a guest were to launch into a lengthy explanation about how difficult it had been to make the cake because she hadn't been feeling very well, but how glad she had been to do it since she is so fond of her hostess. And it would be still worse if a guest who brought such a contribution acted as if she had provided the whole dinner.

The situation is somewhat the same with regard to our offering at Mass. It is good to be able to place a host in a ciborium, when we come into church for

Mass, as a sign of our self-offering to God with Christ and our fellow-worshipers, of our desire to take part in Christ's sacrifice. It is good to put our money in the collection box as another sign of the same desire to give ourselves and everything we have to God in worship and in serving our neighbors' needs. It is good when these material offerings given by all of us are brought up to the altar in procession to indicate their meaning in action.

But it isn't so good to go on about it, either in what we sing or in our own thinking. This is the trouble with most of the offertory hymns now being sung. They try to express the whole theology of sacrifice and, as a result, they are usually unpoetic and banal. But even when they are better poetry, this is not the place to elaborate on our contribution to the Mass.

And the melodies are usually not appropriate either. As Fr. Reinhold says in the Spring, 1965, number of *The Living Light,* the tunes and texts of the antiphon at the offertory "are not meant to go with a popular procession, but to be a very solemn accompaniment to the procession with the gifts. It is not and never was meant to be substituted for by a marching hymn."

It is no wonder, then, that so many of us dislike these offertory hymns and resent singing them. They are the result of some zealous educators' desire to make sure that we really understand that we are offering ourselves and our gifts to God with Christ, and so they annoy us as all over-explaining does. What we should be singing is the sacred equivalent of the guests' "We're glad to be here today," as expressed in one or another mood by the offertory antiphon in the missal (which is meant to be the refrain sung between verses of a psalm). The prayer over the gifts, then, expresses in one way or another the sacred equivalent of "Here are some things we hope you can use." So the offertory antiphon and the prayer over the gifts say all that we need to express in words during the offertory.

We will not, certainly, be "in on" the sacrifice if we don't intend to offer ourselves and everything we have and do to God with Christ's offering. But we should always remember that our self-offering and our gifts are only worthy of God's acceptance because we are members of Christ and he takes them up into his perfect offering. *He* is our real offering to God, with ourselves included in it by God's mercy, as it is by God's mercy that we can offer with him.

This is why the prayer over the gifts so often asks that God make us and our gifts less unworthy of his acceptance, and often that our taking part in Christ's sacrifice-banquet may make us worthier. For it is only because our offerings are taken up into Christ's that "what each of us has offered will be useful for the salvation of all." We may hope, then, that instead of the hymns that distress us, we may be allowed to sing a refrain like the offertory antiphon while the choir sings the verse, and be allowed not to seem so pushy about what we have to give.

Food and Drink

Many churches are now inaugurating the custom of placing tables by the entrances to the aisles with a bowl full of altar-breads and a ciborium. Everyone who is to receive communion places one of the breads in the ciborium, and all the ciboria are solemnly carried to the altar at the offertory. This custom should help us to realize that we have a part to take in the sacrifice (and also that we aren't taking our full part unless we receive communion). But it can't be much more than a gimmick, as soon as we get used to it, unless we realize more than most of us do about the meaning of bread and wine as brought to the altar and used for the eucharist. They mean food and drink; and food and drink mean life itself.

The first obstacle to our appreciating all this is that the altar-breads don't seem like real food at all and, to make things worse, we have been conditioned to treat the consecrated host we receive in communion as little like food as possible. I was given the opportunity, a couple of years ago, to look over the forms filled out by the incoming freshmen at a Catholic college as part of a survey of their religious and social attitudes. They were asked, among other things, whether they considered various actions to be a mortal sin. They disagreed widely on most of the items, but an enormous majority agreed that it is a mortal sin to chew the consecrated host when one receives communion. I was quite startled by this, having been taught myself that one should avoid chewing but nothing about doing so being a mortal sin. However, our young-adult friends said that they had been taught that it was. A mortal sin to do what our Lord said, "Take and eat!" He didn't say, "Take and suck."

This is certainly an illustration of how general Catholic thinking in the Western Church had been going in the direction of a false spiritualizing of our religion until the doctrinal, scriptural and liturgical renewals began to reverse the trend. The bread used for the eucharist was made whiter and whiter and thinner and thinner, as if this would be more fitting material for the eucharist than a good thick chunk of something that would not only *be* bread according to the legal requirements but would also look and taste and chew like real bread. And Catholics were taught that it was in some way wrong to "eat" the eucharistic bread — as if it were somehow more respectful to suck it like a cough drop!

The trouble with all this is that it is precisely the "foodinesss" of bread which is the sign of what Christ does for us in the eucharist, and so makes it a fitting gift for us to place upon the altar. And the same way with the wine; it is because it is real drink that Christ uses it in the eucharist. Few of us in the past were trained to be alert and responsive to this sign-value aspect of the sacraments — that they not only "effect what they signify" but also *signify what they effect*. God wants us to appreciate the "wateriness" of water — what water naturally is and does — and what he has done with it in sacred history, in order to appreciate baptism. He wants us to appreciate bread and wine as food and drink and what these mean in human life, and also what they mean in sacred history, in order to appreciate the eucharist.

Thank God, the "new" catechetics is now teaching children that the altar-breads are really bread and that, after they have become the body of Christ at the consecration, they are meant to be eaten as food. But the rest of us have to work to gain an appreciation of the fact that what is placed on the altar as our gift, what is changed into Christ's body and blood at the consecration, is really meant to be not some ethereal ambrosia and nectar, but real food and drink. For if we don't appreciate the signs of the eucharist, how can we respond to what our Lord means by using them?

Food and Drink

As we mentioned earlier, one difficulty in the way of our appreciating what the bread and wine on the altar at Mass really mean is the fact that the altar-breads usually don't seem anything like real food at all and that we have been conditioned not to *eat* what we receive in communion. And, of course, we never have a chance to drink the wine that has been changed into the blood of Christ (though we may be able to do so in the future since the *Constitution on the Sacred Liturgy* opened up the possibility: "Communion under both kinds may be granted when the bishops think fit, not only to clerics and religious, but also to the laity, in cases to be determined by the Apostolic See").

Of course, this doesn't affect our *knowledge* of the eucharist. We "know" that the altar-breads are bread, that the wine on the altar is a drink; we can study the theology of the eucharist and learn the supreme fitting-ness of these signs for Christ's sacrifice-banquet. But not really eating and drinking does affect our *appreciation* of the eucharist. And the Lord planned the whole "economy" of our salvation, as the Fathers call it, the way he has gone about bringing us to share his life, to reach our whole human selves, not just our minds.

For this reason, I wish that all Catholics could have the experience from which fifteen of us once benefited: a Mass in which there was only one large altar-bread, not a white, round, paper-thin disk, but an inch-thick unleavened whole-wheat roll (like the ones I used to make when I was a young cook and forgot the yeast). The celebrant broke this really bready bread into bite-size pieces for himself and the communicants. My many years of study and theorizing about the eucharist as "food indeed" were not as convincing as this one experience of the bread of life received under the sign of what was clearly bread and nothing else.

Perhaps this kind of altar-bread could be used occasionally for small groups, for small class-celebrations, etc. Certainly, all of us could encourage, in whatever ways are possible, the existing tendency to use thicker altar-breads and, perhaps, also to have them made out of whole wheat — not from any health-food faddism, but because whole-wheat hosts seem a good deal "breadier" than white ones (perhaps because they look and taste quite a lot like some of the various crackers now on the market, which are certainly a normal American kind of food).

Another possibility, to help us appreciate the fact that the bread and wine used for the eucharist are meant to be real food and drink, is to take part in a celebration of the Byzantine liturgy, which uses leavened bread. This is cut up into little chunks like croutons and, at communion time, these are immersed in the consecrated wine and administered to each communicant with a long spoon.

All this may seem to have nothing to do with the essentials of religion. But one of our great difficulties today is that we have located religion out in a region that is neither human nor divine, but in a never-never land somewhere in between. The same mentality has made Christ seem like a kind of superman (or, on the other hand, a baby or a doll), rather than the Son of God who took on a human nature, "like us in all things save sin" and who, now in glory at the Father's right hand, is the "final man" — the exemplar of what God wants real human beings to become. And so, we need to realize how God reveals and gives himself to us in ways that are fully human and divine if we are to respond to him — in the Mass and in our lives — as the human persons we are, growing toward the fully human and Christian persons he wants us to become.

Our Daily
Bread

Fr. Gerald Ellard of happy memory, whom we have quoted before, explained in his book, *The Mass of the Future,* how our altar-breads came to be round and stamped with a symbol, so that they look more like coins than like bread. It took place centuries ago when the people no longer brought the bread and wine for the eucharist but gave money instead, as we do today. And it was in aid of an effort to help the people realize that it was their money that bought the bread. If the people saw that the bread on the altar looked like coins, they would be able to identify their offerings with it.

This sort of thing, however well-intentioned, is not what is needed to help us understand the Mass or our part in it. As we have previously tried to suggest, what we need is rather to grasp with our minds and hearts and imaginations and senses what bread and wine mean, as our Lord and the Church use them in the Mass. We have difficulty in doing so first of all because we have never really appreciated the fact that the bread and wine on the altar are meant to be eaten and drunk. We are suffering from the effects of a long-enduring mentality in the Church that turned away as far as possible from the physical aspects of the sacraments through which Christ conveys their meaning to us in order to concentrate on their effects on us — effects which cannot be fully realized unless we understand what Christ is doing and cooperate with it.

But we also have other problems about appreciating the bread and wine of the eucharist, problems which are the result of our particular civilization. In the Graeco-Roman culture of our Lord's time and in all the cultures which are its heirs (and some others, also) except our own, bread is really the staff of life, the staple food of every day. It may be made out of wheat or barley or oats or some other grain — wheat is usually considered the finest. Other foods may be added to it, but it is the bread that provides the main nourishment. (It is said that a good-sized piece of the dark bread of our Lord's time, with a cup of wine, would provide a well-balanced diet with all the necessary vitamins, minerals, etc.) But we don't think of bread as much more than an accompaniment to a meal; it is only necessary for sandwiches. And so, bread does not mean essential food.

Equally, many ethnic groups in this country do not think of wine as *the* drink, the normal accompaniment to a good meal, the drink that gladdens men's hearts. What, then, can we do to cultivate a sense of what bread and wine mean in holy scripture and Christian tradition?

Our national diversity and the wonders of modern food-processing and marketing can help us here. Things are looking up as regards bread (there was a time when you had to make your own, unless you lived in a big city, if your children were to realize that bread could be something other than a dead-white, tasteless, squashy substance). Many varied and substantial kinds of bread are available now, not only in Italian and Jewish and Polish stores, but also in ordinary supermarkets. And good American wines of many kinds are also easy to come by (some at far lower prices than the materials for highballs and cocktails, for instance).

As part of the liturgical education urged by the *Constitution on the Sacred Liturgy,* then, we might give ourselves and our families a varied experience of different kinds of bread and also of wine, making the connection between what is on our tables and the bread and wine placed on the altar at Mass. Perhaps, then, it will mean more to ourselves and our children when we hear our Lord say, "I am the bread of life."

Our Daily
Bread

Many of us suffer from another and a deeper difficulty when it comes to appreciating the bread and
wine of the eucharist — besides those we have mentioned already — and this is a particular hazard, re-
sulting from our "economy of abundance." We don't
really appreciate food or drink as *necessary to life*. We
have never had to be without either long enough to
realize experientially what they mean in our lives.
Food and drink are almost always available; one may be
uncomfortable on a journey or under some special
circumstances for a while. But most of us really don't
know what it is like to go without food or drink long
enough to really endanger our health or our lives. A lot
of us even have to fight food off by going on diets.

If it is going to mean very much to us, then, when
we place altar-bread in the ciborium on the way in to
Mass and see it taken up to the altar at the offertory,
if it is going to mean what it should to us to receive
the Lord under the sign of bread in communion, we
need to think about food and drink, to take them as
seriously as do our brothers and sisters all over the

world who never have enough for full life and health, who never have enough to keep alive.

We need to realize that God is continually re-creating us through the gifts of his creation which we use as food and drink. The fact that human beings are now, at least to a greater extent than ever before, in control of the natural forces that produce what we need for nourishment does not mean that we are any the less dependent on food and drink to keep alive. Even if science produces perfect food-pills as well as all those liquid meal-substitutes, we shall still have to eat and drink *something*. And it is still God who gives us whatever we have, and gives human beings the ingenuity and wherewithal to make such varied uses of his gifts.

We also need to realize that we re-create *each other* through food and drink — and this is more true in our civilization than ever before. It would be good sometime, at the family dinner table, to consider where all the various foods and spices and beverages come from, and how many people must have been concerned in providing them — from the farmer or herdsman, through all the persons engaged in the complicated food-processing and distributing machinery of modern society, to the wage-earner who makes it possible to buy the food and the cook who puts it on the table. It might be good to pray for all the people whose work has helped to provide this dinner, and also to pray that men solve the economic and social problems which prevent everyone on earth from being properly fed. We could also bring out — and children will be a great help here — what happens when people aren't properly fed, and how many on earth today are not.

All this can help to bring home to well-fed Americans how food and drink summarize, symbolize, stand for both human needs and human efforts — human needs of God's gifts and our neighbors' work, human efforts to use God's gifts for the fullness of human life for everyone. And so, we shall begin more fully to appreciate what the bread and wine on the altar mean, and what we should mean by contributing to placing them on the altar, to be changed into Christ's own body and blood in the Mass and given to us in communion. We are acknowledging our membership in the human race and in the body of Christ, with all that this implies in relation both to God and to our fellowmen.

Many
Become One

I do not know whether anyone has yet produced a film about the Mass which would begin with pictures of wheatfields and vineyards and then show how the grains of wheat are harvested and ground up together to make flour, how the grapes are gathered and crushed together to make wine. But such a film would be very helpful to our understanding of the eucharist. It would help us appreciate one final characteristic of both bread and wine that makes them supremely fitting as the signs of our self-offering to God with Christ and under which the Lord gives himself to us to make us into one body with him.

Our Lord spoke of the grain of wheat that has to fall into the ground and die to its life as a grain of wheat in order to produce many new grains — and spoke of it in connection with his imminent death and resurrection. In the same way, all grains must die — either by being planted as seed or by being ground up into flour, if they are to fulfill their purpose. Our Lord also spoke of himself as the vine, of which we are the branches — branches that are to bear fruit, fruit that is to be made into wine.

As we said earlier, the bread and wine on the altar mean food and drink, which means life itself. But they also mean the laying down of one kind of life in order to give and to gain another. And they mean giving up apartness and separatedness in order to become one. As one of the oldest known Christian prayers, the *Didache,* puts it: "As this bread that is broken was scattered upon the mountains and was gathered together and became one, so let your Church be gathered together from the ends of the earth into your kingdom."

And so, when we take part in the Mass, when we contribute to placing the bread and wine on the altar, when we offer ourselves with Christ and when we receive communion, we are committing ourselves to following Christ in laying down his life to "gather together the children of God that are dispersed." We are committing ourselves to trying to do away with our prejudices, our dislikes, our self or group interests that keep us separated, in one way or another, from our fellow human beings and our fellow Christians. We are committing ourselves to trying to foster in our daily lives that unity in love which was the object of Christ's prayer at the Last Supper, "That all may be one, even as you, Father, in me and I in thee: that they also may be one in us."

But, in making such a commitment, we do not need to fear that the Lord is asking us to become a homogeneous mass. As we more completely become members of Christ's body, we become more ourselves, our true individual and personal selves as God wants us to be. The Holy Spirit who makes us one in love is a fire that burns away whatever makes us less ourselves. Christ came to give us more and truer life, not a diminishing of life. But to gain this life, we must be willing to die daily to our selfishness and self-centeredness. This is what the bread and wine on the altar tell us. This is what our offering of them should mean to us. This is what our eating the bread that makes us one body will effect in us, if we allow it to do so.

Through these signs of bread and wine, then, Christ wants to tell us a great deal about the eucharist. It is to help us understand and appreciate this wealth of meaning that experiments with different kinds of offertory processions are being made, that more substantial altar-breads are being used, that the laity may be allowed on certain special occasions to share the cup as well as to eat the bread in communion. None of these "innovations" are gimmicks. They are attempts to carry out the desire of the *Constitution on the Sacred Liturgy* that the rites should "express more clearly the holy things which they signify."

A Last Word
on the Offertory

I have heard in many different places around the country that some people are really disturbed at the practice of having everyone who is to receive communion place an altar-bread in a ciborium on his way into church to take part in the Mass. It isn't sanitary, they say, to have to receive in communion an altar-bread that somebody else has touched with possibly not-too-clean fingers.

This difficulty reminds me of a cartoon that appeared in the *New Yorker* once, depicting the vicissitudes (including being dropped in the muddy street) which a loaf of French bread had undergone from the time it was taken out of the oven in the bakery until it was brought in on a silver salver covered with a spotless white napkin and placed on the table of an expensive restaurant. If we begin to think about all the possible hazards involved in eating anything except what we have personally cooked and served, we should certainly be reduced to a limited and strictly home-cooked diet.

However, where this practice really disturbs people,

it would seem possible to overcome the difficulty by the simple expedient of providing tongs, like the ones used for lump sugar or small ice cubes. For this gesture of deliberately placing an altar-bread in the ciborium, which will, at the offertory, be brought up with the wine to the altar in some kind of procession, does seem helpful to full participation in the Mass in various ways.

For one thing, it gives us a chance to see the altar-breads and so to be reminded — especially if they are of the more substantial and bready variety now being used in more and more churches — of what this offering of bread means.

Again, when the ciboria filled with the altar-breads are brought up to the altar in procession, we can see that these gifts, this food for our bodies which is to become the bread of life, come from us. They do not appear on the altar from nowhere; they come from us; they have been provided by us. We have identified ourselves with them as they are placed on the altar to become the body of Christ. There the priest receives them and asks, in the prayer over the gifts, that God will accept them and sanctify both them and us through the holy sacrifice.

Thirdly, this placing of an altar-bread in a ciborium by each person who intends to receive communion might help to make it clearer to those who do not yet realize it that one does not fully take part in the Mass unless one receives communion — a fact noted both in the 1958 *Instruction on the Liturgy* and in the *Constitution on the Sacred Liturgy*.

And, finally, this practice might encourage priests to do what is urged in the Constitution, to make it possible for the faithful to receive hosts that have been consecrated at the Mass they are attending, and not at some previous sacrifice. After all, when you take part in a meal and your food has to be brought, as a kind of afterthought, from a refrigerator or a cupboard, you can't help feeling that you weren't really expected, that giving you food was not an integral part of the meal as it was planned. In the same way at Mass, when the celebrant, having eaten the bread and drunk the cup that are on the holy table, has to go and unlock the tabernacle to give the faithful their share of the bread of heaven, it doesn't look as though their participation in the Lord's supper was really planned for; it makes it look like a kind of "extra." The main problem seems to be that of calculating how many altar-breads to consecrate at each Mass; if each person intending to receive communion placed an altar-bread in the ciborium when going into Mass, the difficulty would seem to be solved. So let us hope that this practice spreads — with the use of tongs if necessary to make it acceptable.

IV
PRAISE AND SACRIFICE:
THE GREAT EUCHARISTIC PRAYER
AND SACRIFICE

"While They Were Eating"

Many of the newer books designed to help parents and teachers prepare children for their first communion base their explanations of the Mass on the child's experience of family meals. One may question the wisdom of insisting, as some do, on the *enjoyableness* of family meals — most parents and children do not find the family evening meal necessarily the most enjoyable time of day, especially when father is tired from his day's work and mother is trying at once to serve dinner, feed the baby and keep the other children in order. Nevertheless, liturgists and theologians alike tell us that we will understand the Mass better and take part in it more appreciatively if we see it primarily as a meal, because this was the way that our Lord himself instituted the eucharist.

We have been speaking about the human and Christian meaning of food and drink in general, and of bread and wine in particular. Human experience and holy scripture also have much to tell us about the meaning of meals — not just eating but eating *together*. In every culture and civilization, to eat together is a sign of sharing life. We need food to live; to partake of food and drink from the same table, to share the same loaf of bread and the same drink, means some kind of community of life. To invite a guest to a meal in one's house shows a desire to include him, in some way at least, in the family community. Groups and organizations of all kinds naturally schedule some kind of meal or banquet as the beginning or climax of a year's program of working together.

So it is not surprising that, in the Old Testament, a liturgical meal was prescribed connected with the offering of sacrifices, a meal taken in God's own dwelling, indicating the community existing between God and the faithful Israelites. Again, the prophets and our Lord himself speak of the happiness that God means to give his people in his kingdom in terms of a meal and, more particularly, a wedding feast. For, in the kingdom, we shall share God's life, and share it together. In the accounts of our Lord's resurrection, commentators say that his meals with his disciples are stressed to show us that the promises have been fulfilled and the kingdom has begun.

But one meal above all was prescribed in the Old Testament — the paschal meal, taken family by family, commemorating the great event of Israel's history, the deliverance from Egypt. At this meal, at which the paschal lamb was eaten, there was a special blessing of bread at the beginning of the meal and a very long and solemn blessing of the final cup of wine at the end. But all Jewish meals, especially those of groups of disciples gathered together with their master, included — like Christian meals — some forms of blessings.

Scripture scholars are still discussing whether the Last Supper was actually a paschal meal or a "meal with paschal overtones" (as the *New Testament Reading Guide,* n. 13 puts it). But in any case, it was an already-existing meal liturgy that our Lord used and transformed into his eucharist.

If we are to understand the structure of the Mass, then, we need to see the offertory as the direct preparation for the holy meal when the bread and wine are placed on the table, and to see the great eucharistic prayer, from the beginning of the preface to the final "Amen" at the end of the canon, as the supreme grace or blessing before the meal in which we at once bless God for his gifts to us and draw down his blessing on us, and do so with Christ. Because the celebrant who carries out this great prayer speaks in the name of Christ and repeats his words at the Last Supper, our thanksgiving becomes Christ's own act of praise and sacrifice re-presented here in our midst, and our bread and wine become his body "given for us" and his blood shed for us. And so, the holy meal in which we share by receiving communion not only signifies but really gives us participation in Christ's life, together. "Because the bread is one, we though many are one body, all of us who partake of the one bread."

"Giving Thanks"

All parents have observed how difficult it is to get small children to come up and say "thank you" to someone who has given them a present. In his fine book, *The Psalms Are Christian Prayer,* Fr. Thomas Worden suggests that this phenomenon is due not to thoughtlessness or lack of gratitude, but rather to a greater sensitivity than adults have as to what the situation calls for. Children will much more readily say, "What a cool model!" or "You're the best uncle in the world!" than a direct "thank you" because they feel that praise of the giver and the gift is the best expression of gratitude, rather than a mere *quid pro quo* "thank you." And, Fr. Worden says, the writers of the Old and New Testaments felt the same way, and so does the most authentic Christian tradition. We find little direct thanks of God in the psalms, but a great deal of praise.

Along this same line, scholars tell us that the Greek word "eucharist" doesn't simply mean to "give thanks" but rather to "praise," and that it in turn was a translation of a Hebrew word, *barak,* meaning "to bless" in the sense of acknowledging and praising the Lord's goodness. "To the Hebrew mind, to *bless* anything and to pronounce a *thanksgiving* over it are not two actions but one. It is the thanksgiving, that is to say, the acknowledgment of God's own creative Word made over the things which that selfsame Word had created which fills these things with the heavenly blessing. And from this fact follows the character of consecration which was ascribed to the thanksgiving, to the *eucharist* as pronounced over a meal" (Fr. Louis Bouyer, *Liturgical Piety*).

So we can understand better why the celebrant, before beginning the great eucharistic prayer of the Mass, first invites us to "lift up our hearts." In the language of holy scripture, the "heart" means the profound center of our personality, not simply the focus of our emotions, but of our thoughts and our willing and our deepest decisions. We are invited, then, to lay aside all our preoccupations with ourselves and to get ready with our whole selves to praise and give thanks to God.

This dialogue between the celebrant and the congregation at the beginning of the preface is very important because it brings home to us the fact that we are to take part in the great prayer and act of praise to be offered and carried out in the eucharistic sacrifice. We are not simply to watch, but also to offer, not only through the hands and words of the priest, but also with him. And this dialogue is also important because it sets the keynote for the whole eucharistic prayer, showing us that all that is said and done is, above all, praise of God's goodness and love, which has done and is doing and will do such great things for us through his Son to bring us to share his life, to live as "sons in the Son."

This is why we are now asked, at every Mass and not just at high Masses, to stand up for this dialogue and through the "Holy, holy, holy." Certainly, the former practice where, at low Mass, we simply went on sitting down when the priest said "Sursum corda" didn't make much sense. You don't feel very much as though you were starting on the central action of your whole life, taking part in Christ's great act of praise and sacrifice, when you just keep on sitting. The normal thing to do is to stand when you are called on to start something important.

But, still more, the posture of standing expresses freedom, as the posture of kneeling expresses slavery. The early Christians prayed standing up, except at penitential seasons, for they felt this attitude best expressed the freedom and dignity which Christ had given them, the freedom of sons in their Father's presence.

When we stand up for this dialogue, then, however weary we are, let us try to make both our getting up and our responding to the celebrant a real beginning of praise, joining with the celebrant's words and the great thoughts of the preface. "It is right and just."

"You No Say
What I Mean"

My husband's family, many years ago, employed as a cook a lady from Finland whose grasp of English was somewhat insecure. One of her favorite phrases, used rather despairingly, was, "But you no say what I mean!"

This exclamation somehow seems very apt in connection with various difficulties in communication faced by the liturgical renewal. So many terms, the meaning of which seems quite obvious, were originally meant to mean something quite different — so much so that what we think they mean is positively misleading. The prayer termed "secret" (the prayer over the gifts) is one example. Whatever its origin, which is still disputed, scholars agree that it wasn't meant to mean "hidden" or "to be kept from the people."

But perhaps the most misleading name for a prayer in the Mass is the "preface." A preface, to us, means an introduction that is not an integral part of the book or whatever, but something quite separate and non-essential to the structure of what it precedes. Because the term "preface" came to be applied only to the first part of the eucharistic prayer, generations of Catholics

have naturally thought of it as a kind of solemn introduction to the main business of the Mass and not an
integral part of it.

This mistaken idea has been promoted also by the
way missals — both altar and hand missals — have
been arranged. The various prefaces for different feasts
and seasons may all be given together and followed by
the "Holy, holy, holy," or some of them may be
printed along with the propers they go with. But, except
in some of the very latest missals, a new chapter seems
to be beginning after the "Holy, holy, holy." There is
usually a full-page picture, in fact, on the left-hand side
of the page, and the text starts off again on the right-
hand side with a very fancy capital initial.

Now it seems that the preface and the canon together could quite properly be called the "praefatio" of
the Mass, and they actually were at one time. For the
term doesn't mean "speak before" in the sense of introducing something else, but "speak before" in the sense
of "in the presence of others." Scholars say that it was
a technical term, taken over from pagan worship,
meaning a solemn prayer offered by a priest to set out
in words the meaning of the action he was performing.
(This is why many solemn consecratory prayers such
as the blessing of the water at the Easter Vigil, the
central prayers of ordination, etc., are also called
"prefaces.")

This may, at first sight, seem merely a very mildly
interesting piece of liturgical information. But it makes
a vast difference to one's understanding of the Mass
and to intelligent participation — at least I have found
it so — to realize that the preface-and-canon is basically
a continuous whole, *all* introduced by "Let us give
thanks to the Lord our God." This whole is interrupted

in the canon as we have it at present by the mementos of the living and the dead and the two lists of saints before and after the consecration. But basically it is still patterned on the solemn Jewish table-prayer which our Lord used at the Last Supper and adapted to the "new covenant" he then proclaimed and established.

According to this pattern, God is blessed and praised for what he did for his people in the past, for what he is doing for them here and now, and for what he has promised to do for them in the future — and this becomes a plea that he will complete his work in his people and in the world. It was in this pattern that our Lord inserted the sacramental re-presentation of his redeeming work that actualizes and sums up all God's deeds for mankind and redeemed mankind's response.

When you see the term "preface" in your missal or mass card, then, read "eucharistic prayer" — and let us hope that both the term and the typographical arrangement will be officially changed when the revised rites appear so that future generations of Catholics will be spared this particular misunderstanding.

"Giving Thanks, He Blessed . . . ."

Many years ago, a priest was telling us about a play he was composing to help high school students understand the Mass. He was planning to begin with a scene representing the Last Supper. "And then," he said, "I think I'll have the apostles meeting together after the ascension and saying to each other, 'The Lord said to do what he did at the Last Supper, but how are we going to go about it?' "

That priest's idea of starting with the Last Supper in order to understand the Mass was certainly a sound one. But, by now at least, biblical and liturgical scholarship has traced fairly clearly the major stages by which our present Mass rite developed through the centuries from the Last Supper. It is safe to say, anyhow, that the apostles never had the problem which this play attributed to them.

Solemn festive meals, above all the yearly paschal meal and the weekly sabbath meals, were a regular feature of Jewish life when our Lord lived on earth, as they are today. And at that time it was also usual for a group of disciples to have such meals with their teacher.

The apostles must have taken many such meals with our Lord before the Last Supper, and the gospels also record that they ate with him after his resurrection. They didn't have to invent a ritual for celebrating the Lord's supper after the ascension; they had one already.

The Last Supper, scholars tell us, like all such solemn meals had three main features: the introductory prayer and distribution of bread, the meal itself, and the solemn blessing over the last cup of wine. It was at the beginning of the meal, then, that our Lord took the bread and blessed and broke it and gave it to his disciples, saying: "This is my body. . . ." And it was at the end that he said the solemn blessing over the cup of wine and said, "This is my blood. . . ."

The first Christian communities celebrated what in the Acts is called "the breaking of bread" in the same way, with a meal coming between the consecration of the bread and that of the wine. But very early, even before the year 40 it is thought, the two consecrations were placed together at the end of the meal in the context of one solemn blessing still modeled on the traditional Jewish grace-after-meals.

Later on, and apparently sooner in some communities than in others, the eucharistic celebration was completely separated from a fraternal meal, and usually preceded by a service of readings and prayers like the Jewish synagogue service. It is conjectured that this major change came about mainly as a result of the growth of Christian communities — it simply wasn't practical to serve complete meals to so many participants. This change, in turn, led to a change in the setting for the eucharist: only a table for the celebrant was needed. This way was opened up for the later development of altars and churches bearing no resemblance to tables and dining rooms.

But the main lines of the eucharistic prayer remained the same (up until the 4th century, the celebrant improvised the exact wording). One can trace them now, in the liturgies of East and West, beneath the complex developments and formalizations of later centuries. Presumably the experts who are revising our Roman Mass rites are working to bring these main lines out more clearly once again. A beginning has already been made: the celebrant now says or sings the wonderful final summary of the whole prayer, "By him, with him. . . ." *aloud* at the end of the canon.

The purpose of all this isn't archeologizing. It is, as the *Constitution on the Sacred Liturgy* says, to enable the texts and rites to "express more clearly the holy things which they signify." Obviously, serving a whole meal in connection with the eucharist is not one of the "immutable elements divinely instituted" or the Church would not have done away with it centuries ago. But the meaning of the eucharist, as sacrifice and sacrament, is bound up with its being the celebration of the Lord's supper. We cannot understand and take our part in the eucharistic prayer unless we realize its character as a meal prayer, the supreme meal prayer of Christians gathered together to meet with their risen Lord and eat at his table.

"Giving Thanks,
He Blessed . . . ."

Our older sons are home so infrequently, between school and college and jobs, that we feel quite acutely, when we are all present at a meal, that it is an occasion, a celebration. Not only in the sense that we are glad to be together (a gladness well concealed under hot arguments and minor irritations), but also in the sense that we are celebrating how far we have come, in God's providence, in the long process of helping five persons to grow to mature manhood and of carrying out our own life's work.

Of course, every family meal has something of this character of summing up the past and looking forward to the future. It wouldn't be held at all if husband and wife (and their fathers and mothers back through the generations) had not met and married and had children. The food wouldn't be on the table if the father (and often the mother too, today) had not worked at some job or profession and earned this particular form of daily bread. The kinds of food and drink that are on the table are signs of the family's achievements and perhaps of their racial origins, as well as of the members' likings. And, obviously, eating and drinking under any circumstances is an act ordered to future life and activity.

Something of this wealth of reference to past and future is brought out, for example, in the toasts and speeches at wedding anniversaries: past events are remembered in their present development and future flowering "to the third and fourth generation" in some way anticipated. It would certainly be quite natural, on such occasions, for the head of the family to offer, before or after the meal, an extended kind of grace, blessing and praising God for all his goodness in the past which has brought the family to this present occasion, and asking him trustfully to continue his blessings in the future, to complete the work of his goodness for this family, their society and all mankind.

This precisely is the pattern of the solemn Jewish grace-after-meals which was the original pattern of the eucharistic prayer. It began with praise of God himself and went on to recall his great deeds for his people, especially their deliverance from slavery in Egypt, his giving them his law and making them his own people by the covenant, bringing them to the promised land and giving them its fruits, now on the table. It went on to bless and thank him for life and daily food, represented by the food and drink on the table, and was completed by petitions for the well-being of Jerusalem, for the coming of the Messiah and the final inauguration of God's reign.

This solemn recalling of God's wonderful works was thought of as in some way making them present. Particularly at the Passover feast, the participants were aware of the present celebration as renewing the past, as uniting them with their forefathers in their deliverance from Egypt. And, equally, they felt themselves in some sense anticipating the future blessings of messianic times, when the People of God would share in the great messianic banquet foretold by the prophets.

If you look at our present Roman eucharistic prayer, you can see the same pattern running through the preface (the Easter or Pentecost preface is more typical than that of the Holy Trinity) and sanctus; the consecration; the prayers that God give his blessings to those who partake of the holy food and drink on the altar-table, and that he bring the faithful departed and his servants here present to the fullness of life and joy with his holy ones; and the final petition-praise that, as we receive everything good through Christ, so all honor and glory be given forever and ever through Christ to the Father in the Spirit.

But, in the Mass, the remembrance of the past and the anticipation of the world to come are real in a sense that only Christ can make them. The whole work of our redemption — past, present and future — is really re-presented in the Mass so that we may rejoice in it, share in it more fully, praise God for it and commit ourselves to it. All the meaning that is implicit in human meals, and the deeper meaning of their solemn festive meals to God's people in the old covenant, are fulfilled and realized in the eucharist. When we say "Amen" at the end of the canon, we are saying "Yes" to all this.

Giving Up,
or Making One?

In one of her early books, published many years ago, the English writer Caryl Houselander described how a husband might feel if he came home from his day's work and his wife began to tell him how uncomfortable she had made herself all day, and said that she had done it to show her love for him. "I pricked my finger ten times on purpose when I was sewing. . . . I put salt in my coffee and some pebbles in my shoes. . . ." Surely he would think that his wife had a very odd idea of him and of what would please him. And, Caryl Houselander said, "Perhaps God feels the same way about many of the 'sacrifices' we make in order to please him."

Actually, the biblical idea of sacrifice does not stress the idea of giving up for its own sake, or even of giving up for the sake of getting. The psalms and the prophets keep insisting that the Lord does not need sheep and goats and bulls, and that offering them to him in sacrifice in order to win his favor does not please him at all.

The purpose of all the sacrifices prescribed in the

Old Testament was to bring the people into God's presence, doing away, if necessary, with whatever had caused them to lose it, whatever had alienated them from him. As the bible keeps saying, these sacrifices made no sense unless they were signs of the worshipers' desire to be at one with God by doing his will. What they had to give up, then, was not a sheep or a bullock or whatever, but their own ways that were opposed to his — their idolatry, their lack of justice and mercy to one another. And what they had to give were their "hearts," their desire to live in God's presence and be at one with him.

The sacrifices were signs of this will and desire. In a holocaust, for instance, in which a whole bullock was burned, the idea was to transfer it from the sphere of human life to that of God by turning it into smoke. And many of the sacrifices included a meal taken by the worshipers in the temple as a sign that the Lord had accepted them into his friendship and intimacy.

In many of the sacrifices, also, blood was sprinkled on the worshipers and on the altar. For blood was seen to be a sign of life, the bearer of life, and so in some way peculiarly related to God the creator of life, and fitted both to purify and to consecrate. At the first exodus, for example, the blood of the paschal lamb was used to mark the homes of the Hebrews, thus setting them apart and consecrating them to him. And when the covenant was made on Mount Sinai, after the people had heard God's law and accepted it as the law of their lives, blood was sprinkled both on them and on the altar as a sign of the union of life now existing between God and his people.

All the Jewish sacrifices, in fact, had in view the same purposes as those of the central event in the Old

Testament, the exodus from Egypt — to bring the people out of their state of being far from God, scattered among idol-worshipers, to their life as his own people, living in his presence and by his laws. Every sacrifice was in some way a renewal, a recommitment to the covenant.

When we think about sacrifice, then, we should be thinking along the same lines. By going from our human life through death to his risen life with the Father, our Lord realized everything that all the Old Testament sacrifices signified and attempted to achieve. He brought out human nature into the very life of the Son with the Father in the Spirit. When we take part in the re-presentation of his great "exodus" at Mass, we go with him as his members into the Father's presence — trying to leave behind our sinfulness and self-centeredness that keep us from him.

And when we "make sacrifices" in our daily lives, these should have the same purpose — to bring ourselves and others closer to God. When our giving-up is an act of going-out-of-ourselves, an act of love offered with Christ's great act of love and obedience, then it is a truly Christian sacrifice. God does not like our discomfort for its own sake — only if it brings us out of ourselves and toward one another and him.

Giving Up,
In Order To Give

Several of the new books preparing children for first communion are designed, quite properly, to help the children appreciate the eucharist in terms of a family meal — the family meal of God's children. But in carrying this out, they tend to present the child's experience of a family evening meal, at which all the members are gathered together, as an invariably happy affair, with father so kind and mother so sweet.

Things aren't like that all the time, at least in our house. And one major reason is that father and mother are both so tired. After our day's work to earn the money to buy the food, and the effort of preparing it and getting it on the table, we are usually more or less worn out. We can only hope that our real love for each member of the family will come through the irritability that fatigue too often causes. For, of course, we wouldn't have got involved in all this work and worry if we didn't love the children and want them to grow up strong and healthy.

But seeing family meals as they often are can be as helpful to our appreciating the eucharist as the over-idealized picture sometimes given. The food and drink on the table are at once the effect and the sign of the parents' worn-out-ness. In nourishing the family, the food and drink on the table are actually accomplishing the purposes that the parents are getting worn out *for*. Every meal, then, is, in some sense at least, a realization, a representation of the fact that the parents are laying down their lives little by little, year by year, to help their children attain the fullness of life and maturity.

Christ our Lord laid down his human life, dying on the cross, in order to become, in his risen life with the Father, the "source of life to all who believe in him." He had to die to the "life of the flesh," the limited life of human nature as we know it, in order to live the life of the Spirit and be able to communicate that life to men, to bring human persons to the fullness of life and maturity that God wills for them. And he *does* communicate this life to us, here and now, above all through making himself our food and drink in the eucharist.

At the Last Supper, when our Lord said, "This is my body. . . . This is my blood. . . ." in the context of a table-prayer of praise and blessing, he committed himself to this whole work of laying down his human life in order to be able to give the fullness of life to mankind. He also actually carried out this whole work sacramentally, making himself food and drink for his disciples.

At the Mass, we do not have to wait for the consecration to have our Lord present in our midst, any more than the apostles did at the Last Supper. He has been with us from the outset because we have "gathered together in his name." He has spoken to us through his

Word. He is present in the priest who, at the consecration, speaks and acts in his very Person. But, at the consecration, he makes himself present under the signs of the bread and the wine, as our food and drink. And, in doing so, he re-presents everything that he did in order to be able to give himself to us as our life — the whole work of our redemption.

Most of us were taught to say, "My Lord and my God!" when the bell rings to alert us to the fact that the consecration has been carried out. This exclamation was the apostle Thomas' response of awed recognition of the Person and mission of the risen Jesus, now become "Lord" in his glorified human nature — the Jesus whom he had known as a man among men, whom he had seen going to his death.

We can then repeat St. Thomas' exclamation as an expression of our recognizing by faith not only Christ's presence in the consecrated bread and wine, but also the re-presentation of his whole work for us, in the past, the present and the future, the work he came to accomplish, of giving us life, life in abundance.

What Do We Offer
at Mass?

When a man and woman get married, they offer themselves to one another in the sense that they promise one another a whole lifetime of mutual self-giving, "until death do us part." Each will have to give up various kinds of self-interest and self-centeredness in order to share a real married life and create a climate of love for their children to be brought up in. Each will have to contribute strength and time and talents to help the other and their children toward fullness of life. All this will be summed up and symbolized in the marriage act that makes them "two in one flesh." The marriage ceremony is a mutual self-giving *in promise* through the sign of their mutual consent.

On the other hand, when a man plunges into a stormy sea, for example, to save someone who is drowning, there is no promise or sign involved — he simply offers his life in his action.

At the Last Supper, our Lord "offered himself" to the Father in both these ways at once. By offering the customary prayer of praise for all God's wonderful works for his people and, in this context, carrying out

114

the whole work of our redemption in the sacramental sign of the bread and wine become his body and blood, he at once dedicated himself to this work and effected it.

When we read the New Testament accounts of what our Lord said and did at the Last Supper, this offering aspect does not seem to be very clearly indicated. But there was no need to do so. The context of the whole meal was sacrificial, in the sense that the participants thought of it as a remembering of God's wonderful works for his people, particularly the exodus and the covenant, and a commitment to carry out in their lives the purpose of these works and of all the prescribed sacrifices — to bring God's people together, to live in his presence. When our Lord said, "This is my body, given for you. . . . This is the cup of my blood, of the new and eternal covenant . . ." he was dedicating himself to carrying out the work of our redemption through his death on the cross, and actually carrying it out in its sacramental sign.

So, when the Church celebrates the eucharist, Christ's offering is re-presented: his self-dedication for the love of the Father and mankind to the work of our salvation, and his carrying it out.

Scholars tell us that it was when Christian communities no longer had a vivid awareness of what Jewish ritual meals signified — and a regular meal had ceased to be part of the celebration — that the eucharistic prayer began to stress explicitly the sacrificial aspect of the eucharist. In our present canon of the Mass, the prayer that follows the consecration says: "And so, Lord, we your servants and also your holy people, remembering the blessed passion of Christ, your Son, our Lord, and also his resurrection from the dead and his glorious ascension into heaven, offer to you the holy bread of everlasting life, and the cup of eternal salvation." In these words, the priest states that we are offering to the Father Christ's loving self-giving to carry out the work of our salvation and his carrying it out through his passion, and glorification — both made present in, and signified by, the consecration of the bread and wine.

We can take part in Christ's self-offering thus represented in the Mass because we are his members. And we can also offer ourselves with him in the sense of rededicating ourselves to the terms of the new covenant, recommitting ourselves to laying down our lives to carry out the purposes of his love among mankind. This, of course, is a promise-offering, to be carried out in our daily lives, the offering which Christ's sacrifice enables us to make, which he takes up into his own perfect offering of love. Our present canon says nothing explicitly about our self-offering. But in offering his, we know that we may include our own in it because this is what he wants, to unite us with himself in his offering of love and in the life that is the effect of this offering.

A "Sacrifice
of Praise"?

I once attended a testimonial banquet held in honor
of a doctor who had been forced, for reasons of health,
to retire from a very active practice. Various authori-
ties in his field were present; so were the administrators
of the hospitals and clinics he had worked in. There
were speeches extolling his skillful and selfless service
of his patients and the community, his contributions to
his specialty, and so on.

I was thinking rather uncomfortably how embarrassing all this must be to him. But then I looked away
from the speaker, and round at my fellow-guests at the
nearby tables. I saw several people whom I knew had
been this doctor's patients, and I was rather awed at
the expression on their faces — so eager and outgoing
and glad. One could see that they were not only agree-
ing with everything that was being said about their doctor, but were putting themselves into it, giving it everything they had. When they applauded at the end of the
speech, it was as if they were trying to put their whole
selves into this action, to show their appreciation of
what this man had been to them and done for them.

In daily life, all of us feel this way now and then, when we suddenly see more clearly than usual what is really "special" about someone we love, how much he means in himself, as a person, and how much he means to us. And most of us feel something like this same desire to go out of ourselves in praise of God the creator when we see a glorious sunset, or the sky on a starry night, or the New England woods flaming in the autumn. We want to do something — and yet our appreciation is somehow a doing in itself, an "ecstasy" in the literal sense of going out of ourselves.

When the priest says, at the beginning of the preface in the Mass, "Let us give thanks to the Lord our God," this is the kind of effort we are being called on to make, the effort which we say it is "right and just" for us to make. "To give thanks" is the literal translation of the Latin "gratias agere," itself a weak translation of the Greek word "eucharistein," which has the idea of praise as well as thanksgiving. But even "eucharist" does not express the full wealth of the original Hebrew word which is sometimes translated, in the psalms for instance, as "bless" ("Bless the Lord, O my soul!"). In taking part in offering Christ's eucharist, we are going to try to "go out of ourselves" in an ecstasy of praise, of appreciation of God, the blessed one, and the source of all blessings to us.

Of course, we don't ordinarily feel much like this at Mass. We have to make an effort of faith, rather than feelings. But an awareness of what our "giving thanks" at Mass implies seems helpful in showing us what scripture means by a "sacrifice of praise," and how the Mass is such a sacrifice. In his life-giving death, our Lord went out of his earthly life, through death, to life in the Father's presence, achieving what the Old Testament sacrifices could only signify — man's desire to go out of his state of alienation from God to life with him, in his presence. And, at the Last Supper, he offered this "going" in the context of a great prayer of "blessing" God. As the incarnate Son of God, his infinite appreciation of his Father and of the Father's goodness to men translated itself at once into prayer and into the act of going out of this life to the Father, carried out at the Last Supper in its sacramental sign.

So he enables us to go out of ourselves with him at Mass, and thus to make our whole lives, with his, a "sacrifice of praise." "How shall I make return to the Lord for all he has given to me? . . . I will offer the sacrifice of praise and call on the name of the Lord" (Ps. 115).

The Great
Summary

Some famous scientists, my husband tells me, have pictured the whole universe as having exploded from the primal atom like a gigantic Roman candle — out and out and out — now in the process of falling back to the original center, as the golden sparks from the Roman candle fall back to the ground.

This idea is not so very different, in pattern at least, from the Christian vision of all things going "out" from God in creation and returning to him in obedience and praise. But this vision is on the plane of intention, of love, not of physics. . . . God in his overflowing generosity giving existence and life; angels and men freely returning his love in "ecstasy," a praise, a going out of self toward him. And the primal love is that of God's own inner life — the Father always giving himself wholly to the Son and the Son wholly giving himself to the Father, in the Spirit. The dynamic movement of creation is as it were an extension, on the created plane, of the personal giving-and-returning in love that is the inner life of God.

And, in the Christian vision, the Son-made-man,

the Word-made-flesh, is at once he "by whom all things were made," as we say in the creed, and he through whom all things "return" to God in loving self-giving and praise. By sin, by refusing to join in what C. S. Lewis, in his science-fiction novel *Perelandra,* calls, following the thought of some of the Fathers of the Church, the "great dance" of creation to God's glory, mankind became alienated and disoriented. The Father gave his Son to lead us back; and the Son, freely and lovingly, carried out in our human nature his eternal act of loving praise of the Father, and so broke the bonds of sin and death and restored us to true life.

We are used to thinking of our Lord as God, and as the great gift of the Father's love to us. But we need to realize that he is also the infinite "responder" to the Father's love, the leader of our response and he who makes this response possible.

This whole dynamic pattern of creation and re-demption is the underlying pattern of the Mass: God gives us everything through Christ. The bread and wine represent all his gifts to us in nature; the bread and wine that have become the body and blood of Christ are the effective signs of the whole work of our redemp-tion. And we respond to him through Christ, together with all creation, as almost every preface states. We respond by taking part in Christ's self-giving, with our own included in it.

This is why it is so important that the concluding words of the canon are now at least said aloud — though we could hope that soon the whole canon will be aloud and in English. For these give the second half of a great summary of what the Mass and everything else is all about: "It is through him, Lord, that you unceasingly create all these good things, make them holy, give them life, bless them and give them to us. By him, and with him, and in him, is to you, God the Father almighty, in the unity of the Holy Spirit, all honor and glory, forever and ever."

And this is why it is so important that we say "the great Amen," which follows, loudly and with conviction. *Amen* means, "Yes, I agree; I want to be in on what has been said." It means assent and consent and commitment. We might hope that at this point in the Mass we might say (or better sing) three Amens, to make it easier for us to be fully alert and to put our whole selves into what we are saying. Amen, Amen, Amen!

V
COMMUNION RITES FROM THE
"OUR FATHER" TO THE END OF MASS

We Dare To Say
"Our Father"

The Living Light, the catechetical quarterly which
I help to edit, just received a very interesting report
about some of the difficulties the writer encountered in
teaching religion in the "inner city" of one of our great
metropolitan centers. One of these is the fact that most
of the extant catechetical materials assume that the
children who are going to use them will be middle-class
white suburbanites, living in orderly homes conducted
by well-behaved Christian parents — and so the inner
city children (and a great many suburbanite children
too, one would imagine) cannot relate to the people or
the situations pictured.

Still more basically, the "new" catechetics tends to
assume that every child has a positive and healthy experience of fatherhood on which the religion teacher
can build to help the child realize his relationship to
"our Father in heaven, who loves us." But what is the
teacher to do when, as in an appalling number of cases
in the inner city, a child's experience of fatherhood is
something warped and distorted beyond most suburbanites' imagining?

In the Mass, after the great climax of the final

praise and the "Amen" at the end of the canon, having come into the Father's presence with Christ, we pray the *Our Father*. We begin by saying that it is only because Christ told us to do so that we dare to address God as "Father," to tell him that we want what he wants, and to ask him to give us the means to carry out his will.

The *Our Father* is the prayer, which Christ himself gave us, of confidence, of trust in the Father's love for us and care for us. It is the prayer, still more, of confidence in the relationship that we have to him in Christ, of being "sons in the Son." It is the prayer of confidence that he has given us the Spirit of his Son who enables us to cry "Abba, Father!"

When we say the *Our Father* at any time, and most of all when we say it together at Mass, we are therefore committing ourselves to try to act like children of our Father in heaven, perfect in generous love as he is perfect. And perhaps this indicates how the problem of inner-city religion-teaching — and of all witnessing to Christ in our world — will have to be solved.

People who have never experienced normal human love in their own homes or their own communities will have to experience it from us. People who have experienced it in one or another form will have to see, from the way we love our "neighbors," that the love God has poured out in our hearts is a full human love, perfected and carried beyond its best potentialities. They will have to see from the way we live that, as St. John says, "we have passed from death to life *because* we love the brethren" and that this life is supremely worthwhile.

If we act like the children of a Father who is Love, our neighbors will begin to know what this Father is like. It is as simple as that.

Papal pronouncements in recent years relate the *Our Father* in the Mass to the reception of communion — "Give us this day our daily bread" meaning, above all, give us our eucharistic food. But the signs of the eucharistic bread and wine represent the whole of Christ's redeeming work to give us life, abundance of life. If we are not — in our work, in our relationships with other people, in our lives as members of our society — trying in one way or another to help other people achieve abundance of life, how can we dare ask the Father for our daily bread? But none of us have done this perfectly, so we must always go in to say, "Forgive us our trespasses, as we forgive those who trespass against us, and lead us not into temptation, but deliver us from evil. Amen."

With Our Minds
as well as Our Voices

There were the days, not so long ago, when the congregation didn't say the *Our Father* out loud with the priest at Mass. Then there were the days, after the *Instruction of 1958,* when some congregations said it out loud with the priest in Latin. Some pastors said it was meaningless to their people in this unknown tongue. Other said that their people seemed to enjoy saying it and of course they understood it since they knew it so well in English. Now we all say it in English at every Mass.

But it obviously isn't any use saying it in English, rather than in Latin or Greek or Aramiac or anything else, unless we are trying to mean what we say. The *Our Father* comes at a climax in the Mass. We have come into the Father's presence with Christ. We know that we are admitted to that presence and welcomed because we come with Christ, offering his offering of himself and ourselves with him. And so we dare to say, "Our Father. . . ." Here, above all, we need to try to be aware of what we are saying.

The difficulty is, of course, that we not only suffer

from the distractions that may come at any time (Did I turn the oven off before I left home? ... The sermon was so long that maybe we won't get home in time for the rest of the family to get back to the next Mass. ... Why will people wear hats like that?) but that we have said and do say the *Our Father* so often. The standard penance in confession is still "five *Our Father's* and five *Hail Mary's";* we still are urged to say the same prayers five times for this or that petition. (As Fr. Louis Bouyer says somewhere in his *Introduction to Spirituality,* how much more natural and Christian it would be to come out and ask our Father for what we need, as the Lord told us to — "He who asks, receives ..." — than to repeat this *model* prayer over and over until it is very difficult to say it meaningfully.)

Innumerable commentaries have been written on the *Lord's Prayer* by the Fathers and Doctors of the Church, by saints through the ages, by modern writers. One of the most recent, *We Dare To Say Our Father,* by Louis Evely (Herder and Herder, New York, 1965) I have found to be more than ordinarily helpful in making each phrase really relevant to what is being done at Mass and to what I should do in daily praying and living. We cannot, of course, ever exhaust the depths of meaning in this prayer, through which our Lord taught his disciples how to pray. We need to think about each of them (at some other time than at Mass) and so make our prayer at Mass more meaningful.

"In heaven," for instance. ... Does this mean way up (or out) there where astronauts are aiming to go? Obviously not. "Heaven" is not going to be discovered by space travelers, however far they venture from our earth. As Fr. Evely says, it is the *state* which is God's. When we pray, God "calls us to a state which is his, to enable us to pass from our world to his. . . ." — a state of unimaginable vitality of life and love.

Or how about "kingdom"? Does this mean some kind of a super-organization or world state? Of course not, for our Lord said, "My kingdom is not of this world." It means the complete reign of love, of love that has conquered death, when all creation shall have been "delivered from servitude to corruption into the glory of the freedom of the sons of God."

About "lead us not into temptation," Fr. Evely says that our English translation "is really blasphemous." As if God could wish to "lead" us to do evil! "We must never forget that the Aramaic language has not many shades of meaning. . . . God does not lead us into temptation. He loves. But he does us the honor of not preserving us from everything like those mother-hens who bring up their children in cotton wool." What we are really asking, Fr. Evely says, is not to give way to temptations, but to be enabled to make use of them as a means of access to God, not shutting ourselves up against love, but opening ourselves out to it.

We can do a great deal, then, by reading and thinking and asking our Father to show us what this prayer means, to make our saying of it at Mass really meaningful. But perhaps the best thing to do at Mass is to try simply to enter into its spirit. "Father, we want what you want. Give us what we need so that we can do what you want."

Growing Pains?

All parents of adolescent sons and daughters observe how hard it is to know when and how best to help them — even with as objective a task as getting off to school or college. If you do too much, they won't be learning how to do things for themselves (such as buying their own clothes). If you leave the whole affair to them, something essential may be forgotten (such as blankets — we just mailed a package, hoping that our son isn't freezing in the meantime). Still more important, if you do too much, they resent it and think you are treating them like children. But if you do too little, perhaps they will think you don't care.

Such problems don't arise, of course, with small children. They have their urgings toward independence, yet, basically, they realize that they couldn't make it on their own. But an adolescent sometimes is sure he can and sometimes certain he could not. He is somewhere on the long road between the total and unthinking dependence of a baby on his parents, a dependence that expects everything from them, and the freely-recognized dependence of an emotionally mature person on those he loves — a dependence that is the other aspect of the free gift of his love. When your son begins to treat you as a person from whom he is not ashamed to ask for needed help, you know that he is beginning to grow up.

Many theologians and others are now beginning to think that perhaps the whole human race is involved in a development similar to that of a child to an adult, and that we are now, as it were, in the adolescent stage with regard to our relationship to God. One reads many articles and books about "secularism" to the effect that modern man now believes that he can make it on his own; he has no need of God; he can take care of his own affairs and not have to run to God for help when things go wrong.

Some modern secularists would certainly say, for instance, that the *Our Father,* and the prayer that follows it in the Mass: "Deliver us, Lord, from all evils, past, present and to come . . ." are prayers of childish dependence, unworthy of mature persons. In fact, they would say such prayers show that religion is still preventing people from going ahead and really working to do away with the evils of our world; too many people still expect God to do it all.

Such statements may sound blasphemous to Christian ears. But might not this attitude of independence toward God be the equivalent of the adolescent's impatient, "Let me alone; I can manage myself," and so be, at least potentially, a step on the road toward a mature human attitude toward God that would not expect him to do what we ourselves can and should be doing, but would gladly acknowledge our total dependence on him in love?

We Christians, then, need to cultivate this attitude and show our world how fully worthy of mature human persons it is. We can, and many of us do, pray with the childish self-regarding attitude of a baby who expects his parents to see that things go right for him and complains loudly when they do not. Or, because God "has sent the Spirit of his Son unto our hearts," we can pray with the mature attitude of "sons in the Son" toward their Father, sons whom he has invited to cooperate with him in his great work of delivering mankind from all evils and "slavery to corruption" into the "glorious liberty of the sons of God." We can pray, not that he will give us what we want, but that he will enable us to carry out what he wants; not that he will do our work for us, but that he will give us what we need to carry out the work which is ours and his; not that he will do what we should be doing in working for social justice and human betterment and development, but what we cannot do. And this is to deliver ourselves or anyone else from our alienation from God and from one another and within ourselves which is the basic cause of all other evils. This is what Christ has delivered us from — and what we always need to pray to be delivered from more completely — to be delivered from self-centeredness, to be freed for love.

The Breaking
of Bread

It used to be a solemn moment, in my childhood, when my father started to carve the Sunday roast. (Would he remember who liked well-done and who liked rare? Would I get the piece I wanted?) It is somewhat the same in our family today, only the children speak right out and *say* what they want, which we never would have dared to do in my youth. The modern way saves a lot of worrying, and the essential is still preserved: that the father of the family, who has earned the food, now shares it with those he loves.

In our Lord's time, at solemn meals, the father or leader took a special loaf of bread, at the beginning of the meal, offered a thanksgiving blessing over it, and then broke it in pieces and gave each participant a share. This is what our Lord did when he fed the crowd in the desert. "And when he had ordered the crowd to recline on the grass, he took the five loaves and two fishes, and looking up to heaven, blessed and broke the loaves, and gave them to his disciples, and the disciples gave them to the crowds" (Mt. 14, 19).

This is what he did at the Last Supper: "And while they were at supper, Jesus took bread, and blessed and broke, and gave it to his disciples, and said, "Take and eat; this is my body." And this is what he also did when he had supper with the two disciples at Emmaus, after his resurrection, when they "recognized him in the breaking of the bread" (Lk. 24, 30-35), and with the disciples at the lake of Galilee (Jn. 21, 9-14). No wonder, then, that the celebration of the eucharist is called, in the Acts of the Apostles, simply "the breaking of the bread."

Now that, in many churches at least, the priest faces the congregation to celebrate Mass, we can see him carry out this part of doing what Jesus did at the Last Supper, just before saying or singing: *Pax Domini sit semper vobiscum* — "May the peace of the Lord be always with you."

Now, the priest simply breaks the big host into three pieces and puts one into the chalice. But, in the days when the people brought offerings of bread, in the form of small loaves, to be used for the eucharist, the "breaking" was much more of a business, begun by the celebrant and then carried on by the assisting priests, until all the communicants were given their share of the bread of eternal life.

It was in connection with this rather lengthy proceeding, scholars tell us, that the chanting of "Lamb of God, who take away the sins of the world . . ." was introduced into the Mass to give the people something to sing while the breaking of the bread was going on. This is the first prayer, since the eucharistic part of the Mass began, in which we address our Lord rather than the Father; it serves much the same purpose, of lovingly acknowledging his special sacrificial presence in the eucharistic bread, as do the priest's genuflections and raising the host after the consecration, or his holding up the host and saying, "Behold the Lamb of God . . ." before giving us communion.

When we watch the celebrant breaking the host, then, we should see him here, too, acting in the very person of Christ, now breaking the bread that he won for us by his going to the Father through his death and glorification — breaking the bread so as to share it with us, with all his own. And his gesture should bring home to us our duty, in one way or another, to break bread for all our human brothers, to share what we have, to pass on what the Lord has given us, until, as at the Lord's feeding of the five thousand, all eat of the good things that the Lord has provided, through creation and through redemption, and until, as at Emmaus, all men can "recognize him in the breaking of the bread."

Signs
of Unity

At Mass once, in a small church, I heard a child, who was quite close to the altar and watching everything the priest was doing with rapt attention, whisper loudly as the priest broke the host and then dropped a piece into the chalice, "What's he doing, Mother, dunking it?"

This "commingling," after the priest says "The peace of the Lord be always with you," is certainly one of the least easily understood gestures in the Mass as we have it now. Originally, scholars tell us, at a papal or episcopal Mass, the pope or bishop would send, by acolytes, a particle of the eucharistic bread consecrated at his Mass to the priests of the vicinity and each would drop this particle, called the *fermentum,* into his chalice at this point in the Mass. This custom was an expression of the unity of the Church in each diocese, and of the fact that the eucharist is the bond of unity of the Church, and that "all the People of God subject to a bishop should, if possible, be gathered around that bishop's altar and receive the sacrament from his table of sacrifice" (Jungmann, *The Mass of the Roman Rite*). It is also thought likely that at one time in the

Roman liturgy, the pope would drop into the chalice a particle from the bread consecrated at the previous day's Mass, to show that each Mass is always Christ's eucharist, the same Mass yesterday and today.

It certainly isn't much of a substitute to have the celebrant drop into the chalice a particle of the host he has just consecrated at this Mass. But at least we can understand and think about its original meaning.

A modern sign of unity, which seems to be very meaningful to priests, is the new rite of concelebration in which many priests take part, all saying the preface and the greater part of the canon together, and taking turns saying the other canon prayers, and all making gestures to show that they are truly concelebrants. The ancient rite of the *fermentum* indicated that although there are many celebrations of the Mass, there is only one sacrifice, Christ's eucharist. Concelebration indicates that although there are many celebrants, there is only one priesthood, Christ's, and only one sacrifice.

The problem, it seems to me, with the present form of concelebration is that it leaves the congregation feeling "excluded." A properly celebrated modern Mass with one celebrant, when the congregation feels in some way gathered round the table of Christ presided over by his representative, engenders a real sense of unity — as did the ancient episcopal Mass celebrated by the bishop, assisted by his priests, with the congregation also gathered around the one table and the one "president." But this modern form of concelebration makes a layman in the congregation feel not that he is taking part in the holy meal of God's family, but that he is watching a kind of head-table procedure in which he has no part. This sense is particularly acute when one is watching the concelebrants taking turns in drinking from the chalice. One feels that this would be a very appropriate form of celebration for a small monastery or a priests' retreat — but not for a Mass in which a congregation is taking part.

Yet we do need some kind of meaningful sign of the fact that the eucharist is always Christ's eucharist, always one and always the bond of our unity, wherever and by whomever celebrated. We need some sign to help us realize, at every Mass, that we are one with our fellow-Christians in a unique way when we are taking part in the eucharist, that we are all gathered around Christ, our priest and leader, drawn closely together in the unity of his love, responsible for one another and for building up the one body to which we all belong, all who partake of this one bread. It will be interesting to see how the revision of the rites takes care of this need.

The Peace
of the Lord

This chapter is being written just after hearing the pope's great address to the Assembly of the United Nations. Certainly, no one can have any further doubts as to what the vicar of Christ thinks about the U.N. and the necessity for fostering peace on earth through peaceful means. And no one can doubt either that each of us can do something to promote peace on earth as persons, as citizens and as neighbors. For, as the pope said, the work of peace-making must go on everywhere, on every level of community, national and international life.

When we hear the word "peace" in a religious context, many of us think that it means primarily a comfortable feeling of security in our relations with God. When at Mass, for instance, after the *Our Father* and before the "Lamb of God," the celebrant says to us, "May the peace of the Lord be always with you," and we answer, "And with your spirit," we tend to think (if we think about it at all) that the peace asked for here is that kind of good religious feeling that one sometimes has when one has been to Mass and received communion.

Of course, real peace consists above all in our having been rescued from our state of alienation from God and made at one with him by our Lord's death and resurrection. Christ *is* our peace, as St. Paul says, since he has brought us to God and made us at one with him — and also at one with one another in him.

But the peace we have been given in Christ as a free gift of God's love has to be communicated to others and to every level of human life. In the Old Testament, peace is promised as the great blessing of messianic times. "And he shall judge the Gentiles, and rebuke many people: and they shall turn their swords into ploughshares, and their spears into sickles; nation shall not lift up sword against nation, neither shall they be exercised anymore to war. . . . They shall not hurt or kill in all my holy mountain."

But this promised peace is to be much more than the absence of war. It is to be the abundance of all good things needed for the fullness of human life in society. "I will bring upon her as it were a river of peace, and as an overflowing torrent the glory of the Gentiles." "The mountains shall yield peace to the people and the hills justice. . . . Justice shall flower in his days and profound peace, till the moon be no more. On the tops of the mountains the crops shall rustle like Lebanon; the city dwellers shall flourish like the verdure of the fields."

This is what the pope pointed out when he praised the work of the U.N., not only in trying to make or keep peace in the sense of the absence of war, but to make justice and truly human living a reality all over the world. We Christians have been given "the peace of Christ that surpasses understanding" as a gift from "the God of peace," as St. Paul calls him. We, more than anyone, have a duty to foster peace, in this full human sense, in our families, our communities, our world. Working for civil rights, working for urban renewal, working against poverty and injustice — all these are works of peace, works proper to the peacemakers whom Christ calls blessed, for they shall be called the children of God.

When, at Mass, we hear and respond to the priest's greeting, "May the peace of the Lord be always with you," let us pray that we may deserve this peace by trying to radiate it, to foster it, to work for it. In scripture, peace and justice always go together. We must be working to make them both realities in our society and our world if we ourselves are to live in Christ's peace.

Needed — A Sign
of Our At-one-ness

Fr. Gerald Ellard, one of the great pioneers of active participation in the liturgy, once remarked that the only directive the Lord gave us about preparation for Mass was this: "If thou art offering thy gift at the altar, and there rememberest that thy brother has anything against thee, leave thy gift before the altar and go first to be reconciled to thy brother, and then come and offer thy gift." Perhaps, he said, as we begin to take the Lord's words more seriously than most of us tend to, we shall have people hurriedly leaving Mass at the offertory who have just remembered that they needed to take care of this essential prerequisite for participation.

But assuming that we have taken pains to be as fully reconciled to everyone as possible before coming to Mass, we still need some kind of outward gesture at Mass of our Christian affection for our fellow-Christians, of our positive desire to be more and more at one with each other. The primary grace of the eucharist is, precisely, the increase of this living and dynamic unity of the members of Christ.

We need to show that we are aware of this eucharistic reality and want to cooperate with it. For we human beings naturally tend and need to express outwardly what we are feeling inwardly. When we are worried, we pace the floor or chew our fingernails. When we are irritated, we have a hard time — even with the help of Anacin — not to express our feelings in shouts or door-slamming. And when we feel a great affection for another person we want to do something to show it.

This sense of a need for a demonstration of Christian affection at Mass, as the sign and seal of participation in the eucharist, was the origin of the ceremony of the kiss of peace, still carried out at high Mass (and in many monastic Masses). After the celebrant has said the first of the prayers before communion, asking for the peace of unity of the Church, he kisses the altar and then goes to the deacon and embraces him in what seems to most Americans a rather artificial gesture; the deacon then similarly "gives the peace" to the subdeacon, and so on, until everyone in the sanctuary has been included.

In the ancient Church, the kiss of peace was exchanged all through the congregation (at that time, the men all sat on one side and the women on the other, so there was no worry about impropriety). In some places this was done at the end of the prayer of the faithful, before the offertory. Later, it was moved so that the peace-giving began when the celebrant said the "Pax Domini," and now, in our Roman rite, it takes place just before communion.

Various experiments have been tried out recently to work out a practical and meaningful gesture that would serve us, in our culture, as the formal "kiss of peace" served the ancients. I once heard of a wedding-Mass where a handshake was used. The only trouble was that the person nearest the server, who had to be the first to hand on the Lord's peace by this gesture, came late and didn't hear the instructions, and was thoroughly bewildered when he was approached by the server with hand outstretched.

Still better, perhaps, than the usual handshake is a gesture I have seen used in various Masses with small groups. The person on the receiving end holds out his hands together, and the person giving the peace-gesture takes them between his hands for a warm and cordial handshake. It would seem as though it would be quite practical to have this gesture passed down from the celebrant, after he has kissed the altar, to the server and so to the congregation. Or if this took too long, everyone could simply carry it out at once with his nearest neighbor.

Anyway, let's hope that the revisions allow for some gesture to show that we really do love one another in Christ.

Standing Up
like Free Men

Many people, it seems, are still bothered by the idea of standing up to receive communion. But perhaps it would be more accurate to say that they are disturbed by not kneeling to receive communion. The new practice seems to be disrespectful, an omission of a fitting sign of respect for the sacramental presence of Christ.

In our parish, the practice of standing rather than kneeling at communion was introduced from the strictly practical angle. Our pastor said that he had observed how painful it was for some of his older and arthritic parishioners to kneel down at the altar rail, and how few of them managed to do it gracefully. Since standing up to receive communion is now allowed and encouraged, he said, you are all going to stand from now on.

I appreciate this approach myself because various operations and ailments make my own kneeling far from an easy or beautiful performance and, so far as I know, none of my fellow parishioners objected to the new practice. But there are other reasons, traditional and theological ones, that make standing a positively appropriate posture for receiving communion and also for taking part in the canon (also now customary in some places).

Today, we do not ordinarily kneel except to pray, and so the attitude of kneeling is associated primarily with prayer. But in the ancient world people did a great deal more social kneeling, so to speak, than we do. Subjects knelt in the presence of their king, slaves before their masters, petitioners before the powerful person who could grant them a favor. And so the kneeling posture seemed to the early Christians very appropriate for penitential and pleading prayer, on days and during seasons of penance.

But, since Christians have been redeemed from slavery to sin and made God's beloved children, they can come into his presence as free men, not slaves. And so the attitude of standing to pray seemed to the early Christians an act of praise of God's goodness, an act acknowledging the reality of Christ's victory over sin and death and their share in it by baptism and the eucharist. Therefore they did most of their praying standing up, especially when taking part in the eucharist. Standing was, in fact, at one time obligatory during the Easter season. (We still have a relic of this in the custom of standing up to say the "Queen of heaven, rejoice" three times a day during the Easter season instead of kneeling to say the Angelus.)

The present reintroduction of the custom of standing rather than kneeling during the canon and when receiving communion is meant, then, to renew our sense of the dignity and freedom of our Christian vocation. It is meant to give us an opportunity to practice the joyful confidence and ease we should have as Christians in the presence of Christ. It is meant to allow us by our very posture to praise God's goodness in making us his children and inviting us to his table.

When we think of it this way, it is obvious that

the new way of doing things does not imply any lessening of the reverence and awe we owe to Christ present in the eucharistic bread. On the contrary, it implies the awestruck recognition of the fact that we creatures, through Christ, have been given the liberty of God's house and can be at home in his loving presence. Our Lord said to the apostles at the Last Supper, "I no longer call you servants, but friends." He says the same thing to us through the Church today.

When we stand to receive communion, then, we should be doing so as a positive gesture of praise and thanksgiving for the "freedom wherewith Christ has made us free."

The Body of
Christ! Amen!

As there are accidental advantages to the custom
of standing rather than kneeling to receive communion,
so there are to the new formula, "The body of Christ!"
to which we respond, "Amen." For one thing, it must
be a good deal easier for the priest distributing communion to say such a short phrase meaningfully over
and over again rather than the long formula, "May the
body of our Lord Jesus Christ preserve your soul
into life everlasting. Amen." For another, since we have
to answer, "Amen," we don't have to look nervously
down the altar rail as the priest comes nearer, wondering just when to open our mouths and get our tongues
ready, and sometimes feeling very silly with our open
mouths when the priest delays for a second or two
at the person ahead of us, or has to go back to the
altar to get another ciborium. We can just wait peace-
fully until he gets to us.

But there is another, and deeper, advantage to the
new formula in that it calls for an individual and
personal response. We do not now come to the altar
rail like small children who are simply going to have

something given to them, who are simply being fed. We are coming like human and Christian persons to whom a gift requires a response, to whom Christ's total gift of his body "given up for us" means our effort totally to respond in self-giving to him and to what he asks of us.

When the priest says to each of us, "The body of Christ!" he is summing up for us everything that the eucharist means and should mean to us — Christ's self-giving in his sacrifice to free us and bring us with him into the Father's presence with the gift of the Spirit, to gather us together into a community of love with one another and with God.

And when we say, "Amen," we are not only making an act of faith in Christ's sacramental presence. We are saying that we agree to receive this gift and allow it to transform us into true Christians, persons who give themselves to others in loving service in order to give them life in some way, as Christ is now giving himself to us to give us life. We are saying that we will try to cooperate with the working of the Spirit in ourselves, and in our world, to build up the body of Christ in love. We are saying that we pledge ourselves to carry out Christ's work in our world, to help free people from every kind of slavery to needs and pressures and oppression, to give all men the opportunity to attain human fullness of life and the still more intense life that Christ came to give us all.

Our "Amen" at communion, then, is not a mere formula; it is a promise. We are pledging ourselves to take part in Christ's sacrifice, to give ourselves, our time, our effort, our energy, in love for our fellowmen, as he is here giving himself in love to us as our food. And we are promising to try to live as members of the community of life and love established among all those who are one body because they eat the one bread. We are giving ourselves up to the workings of Christ's love which makes us all one, and at one, in the Spirit.

Many of the postcommunion prayers express this idea in one way or another. But perhaps this one, from the 15th Sunday after Pentecost, most beautifully sums up what the Lord's gift and our cooperation with it should bring about in each of us: "May the working of this heavenly gift, O Lord, we pray, take hold of us, mind and body, so that our own notions and wishes may not prevail in us, but rather its effectiveness." Amen!

Singing at
Communion Time

In 1955, we happened to be living near Conception Abbey, in Missouri, one of the few places in the United States where the "new" Holy Week rites were tried out previous to the general renewal of 1956. It had been a long and hard winter leading up to that Holy Week. But we felt that it was all worthwhile to have had the privilege of taking part in that first truly vigil-like Easter Vigil. It was in the middle of the night, which truly seemed to be the holy night of the exodus and the resurrection. The light of the paschal candle truly seemed "the light of Christ." The parishioners really felt "included in" the celebration with the monks and the seminarians; we felt ourselves all one in the joy of our risen Lord.

The high point was at communion time, when everyone — the monks in their habits, the white-robed seminarians, the parishioners — started to stream toward the altar, all singing. We were experiencing an anticipation of the fulfillment of Isaiah's prophecy: "And now they that are redeemed by the Lord shall come into Sion singing praises. . . ." We felt united in our singing as a sign of our union through the eucharist, a dynamic and joyful reality.

Again, years later, at one of the Masses during the liturgical week in Cincinnati, when I was coming back from receiving communion, singing with everyone else, it happened that, one after another, I recognized dear friends whom I had not seen for years, whom I had worked with in one or another capacity — all going to or coming from receiving communion, all of us singing together. And here again, our singing seemed to be what it is meant to be — a dynamic bond of unity expressing and fostering our unity in Christ.

Some people seem to have great problems about singing at communion time. Perhaps this is because they have never had such really happy experiences of such singing and never been able to realize that it can be a real expression of the reality of the eucharist, our oneness in Christ. Of course, when the hymn being sung is sentimental or banal, or when nobody is singing with enthusiasm, it is hard to see how the singing could serve any good purpose. Also, of course, if you aren't familiar with the hymn and have to carry a card or book with you up to the altar rail, this can be rather distracting.

But when the hymn is a good and appropriate one — for instance, "Lord, Who at Thy First Eucharist," or "Come to the Banquet," or "Father, We Thank You" — the words are what one would want to be saying to the Lord anyway. (I find them much better than anything I would be thinking on my own.) And one has the joy of singing them to the Lord and singing them with everyone else present, sharing in their devotion and their joy. A hymn in which the congregation sings only the refrain, leaving the verses to the choir or a cantor, can be a solution in places where congregational singing has not yet become easy and not self-conscious. Any group of people can manage "God Is Love" from Fr. Rivers' *An American Mass Program,* and sing it happliy and reasonably well.

But perhaps, if singing at communion time is to become what it can and should be, it will prove necessary in many cases to introduce it in Masses for small groups of people who already have some sense of their at-one-ness in Christ, who are working together to know Christ better and to make him known. In some places, Mass is now being celebrated in people's homes on weekdays, bringing the Mass into a neighborhood within a parish. Such Masses might be occasions where singing at communion could come into its own, as also Masses for other small groups. Then when the same people come to the parish Sunday Mass, they will be ready to take part in the singing for what it is meant to be — the joyful praise of Christ who makes us one body as we share the one bread.

Room for
Improvement

Few people would quarrel with the statement that the present translation of the formula before the final blessing of the Mass is not a happy one. When the celebrant has said, "Go in peace; the Mass is ended," our response, "Thanks be to God," seems like a cry (or sigh) of relief that something rather tedious is now finished and one is free to go away. We may hope that with the revision of the rites and a new translation some more fortunate wording may be given us. My husband argues for "With thanks to God" as being much closer to the sense of the Latin and to its Christian implications.

In the meantime, perhaps, what scholars have to tell us about the origin of the formula will help us to say it as it is meant to be said — not with relief, but as an acknowledgment that we realize that the eucharistic assembly is now dismissed and that we are to live in its spirit of sacrifice and praise as we go out into our work and occupations.

It seems that, in early Christian times just as today, every formal assembly, religious or otherwise, closed with some definite formula of dismissal, and among these, scholars believe, was the Latin, *Ite, missa est,* meaning, "Go, it is the dismissal." The fact that this formula has been among those used from the earliest times in the Roman liturgy is, in fact, a powerful argument for the early Christians' sense of actively participating in the liturgy. People who come to something merely to watch passively do not need to be formally dismissed — they can drift away at any time without excusing themselves; they go away when the show is over. But people who have come to take active part in a meeting feel a need for some sign that the work they have come to do has been done and they are now free to leave. Roberts' *Rules of Order* and common custom call for a motion that the meeting be adjourned and a vote accepting the motion as the conclusion of any formally organized meeting.

"Go, the Mass is ended," is, then, simply this kind of formal proclamation that the Christian assembly has carried out the great work it came together to do; we are now free to leave. Why should we answer, "Thanks be to God"? Josef Jungmann, S.J., in *The Mass of the Roman Rite* tells us: "The dismissal in the Roman Mass is given emphasis and at the same time a religious framework by being introduced with the *Dominus vobiscum* and answered by the *Deo gratias* of the people. In substance, the *Dominus vobiscum* merely takes the place of the vocative of address which might otherwise precede the imperative *Ite*. The *Deo gratias* with which this announcement is answered is an exact parallel to that which the people (according to the liturgical sources of the early Middle Ages) used to answer the announcement of the coming feast days. It is therefore only an acknowledgement that the message has been received, but is imbedded in that fundamental Christian sentiment of thanksgiving.

The last phrase would seem to be the important one for us to think about. As was said earlier in this book, the word "eucharist" which is usually translated "thanksgiving" has much wider connotations of praise, of "blessing" the Lord for his goodness, a blessing that at once praises him for and calls down his blessings on us. This is the attitude with which we are to go out to our living and working, having taken part in Christ's eucharist. We are to share in Christ's redeeming work, laying down our lives in the loving service of others, sacrificing ourselves for our brothers after his example. But we are to do this as a "sacrifice of praise" — praise of God our Father, offered in and with Christ, in the spirit of joyful love. And this is the reason why, after the final blessing, we should go away singing, aloud and in our hearts.

VI
A BEGINNING,
NOT AN ACHIEVEMENT

What
Really Matters

One of the newspapers for whom I write a column
has sent on to me some letters, two of them objecting
somewhat strongly to my way of trying to explain
the reasons for the changes in the liturgy, as well as
objecting to the changes themselves. As to the tone
of my writing, I can only say that I have certainly not
meant it to sound "smug." Because of my friends and
my work of translating and editing books about the
liturgy, I have been given special opportunities during
the last thirty years to learn about the reasons for the
present changes and also to look into the causes of
my own resistance to some of their implications. All
that I have been trying to hand on here is what I have
learned from the real scholars and experts.

As to the changes themselves, there seem to be two
levels of objections, neither of which is clearly dis-
tinguished from the other in the writers' minds: the
deep down objection to the very idea of being "active"
with the other people at Mass, and a distaste for the
actual way things are being done at Mass.

Concerning the first, the question may be put in

this way: Is the Mass meant to be a holy *space of time* during which we are in a holy place where something holy is going on, a space which we can fill in any holy way that appeals to us — as by saying the rosary, following our missal, or just being quiet with God? Or is the Mass meant by God to be a holy *action,* or series of actions, in which we are meant to take part?

Now, it isn't "those liturgists," but Christ himself in his life on earth and in his Church that made the celebration of the eucharist a holy series of actions in which all present are meant to take part in various ways. At the Last Supper, the disciples assembled, they listened to the Lord, they sang psalms as part of the meal-ritual and they followed our Lord's "giving thanks" before he said, "Take and eat. This is my body. . . . Take and drink; this is the new covenant in my blood." Then they ate and drank this bread and wine, and sang more psalms. And so, through the centuries, as the *Constitution on the Sacred Liturgy* says, "the Church has never failed to come together 'to celebrate the paschal mystery': reading those things 'which were in the scriptures concerning him,' celebrating the eucharist in which 'the victory and the triumph of his death are again made present' and at the same time giving thanks 'to God for his unspeakable gift' in Christ Jesus, 'in praise of his glory' through the power of the Spirit."

All these actions — coming together, reading or listening to what is read, celebrating, giving thanks and praise — are actions of body, mind and soul, social actions which people are meant to perform together. They are actions in which all the members of the Church are meant to take part.

Most of us were certainly brought up to think of

the Mass as a holy space of time, to be filled up more or less as we would, not as a series of actions in which we were to join together. But now the Church is calling on us to realize more clearly what the eucharist essentially is and to take our part in it as that. It may be hard to change our ways, but surely, if only as a matter of loyalty, we must try to do so.

It is also true that this present transitional stage in the way in which these holy actions are to be carried out isn't very satisfactory at best, given the mixture of Latin and English, the present state of Catholic hymnody, and so on. And it can be — it often is — made still harder to take by the particular manner in which things are done in some parishes where there is no enthusiasm for participation, or where there is enthusiasm of the wrong sort, where things are done either mechanically or affectedly. But it would obviously seem to be our duty to try to take our part in the celebration as well as we can, and to be patient with what we do not like at present. After all, however poorly the celebration is carried out, we are hearing Christ and taking part with him and with one another in his sacrifice-banquet of praise — and this, of course, is what really matters.

Dreams
Come True?

During a recent liturgical week, many people remarked how happy all the pioneers who attended the first liturgical week twenty-five years ago, also in Chicago, must now be at seeing their dreams come true. Those who said this to me seemed quite surprised when I said that I didn't think that anyone connected with the Liturgical Conference, which has been putting on these annual national liturgical weeks since 1940, feels that its work is done or that his dreams have come true. On the contrary, most of us agree in feeling that the real work is just beginning.

True, it is much more comfortable to attend meetings held in the Conrad Hilton than in a church basement. It is encouraging to have watched through the years the attendance at the liturgical weeks grow from the original 200 to the thousands that have been coming the last few years. Far more deeply, it is wonderful to have lived to see the ideals and ideas for which we have been working authenticated by the highest teaching authority of the Church, to see the "liturgical movement" — once considered the fad of a few discontented unrealists — taken up into the liturgical renewal set out in the *Constitution on the Sacred Liturgy*.

But there are two different things involved in the liturgical renewal called for by the Constitution, and neither of these has by any means yet been achieved. The first is the revision of the rites so that they will "express more clearly the holy things which they signify; the Christian people, so far as possible, should be enabled to understand them with ease and to take part in them fully, actively, and as befits a community." The changes introduced as yet are only preliminary steps. The present Mass, for instance, is very clearly a liturgy-in-transition, not a consistent whole. No one is content with it; it isn't meant to be something to be contented with. The purpose of these changes is to begin working in the right direction while the conciliar commission is carrying out a complete revision of the rites.

This aspect of the renewal is not the business of the Liturgical Conference, but of the hierarchy and those whom they appoint. The Conference is a completely unofficial body, set up twenty-five years ago to promote understanding and appreciation of the Church's worship. (Anyone may join it, and it very badly needs more members to give it the resources it needs to carry on its work. Its address is 2900 Newton St., N.E., Washington, D. C. 20018.)

But the other aspect of the renewal is very much the Conference's business — the "liturgical education" of priests and people alike for which the Constitution repeatedly calls. This work of education is, of course, primarily the responsibility of our bishops and pastors. It is also every Catholic's responsibility, insofar as he can give himself the needed liturgical education and help others to do so by reading, thinking and discussing.

The task of the Liturgical Conference is to help in this work by whatever means and methods may be most effective. It has been doing so by holding the annual liturgical weeks, acting as a resource to diocesan liturgy commissions, organizing institutes, and providing speakers for meetings and reading materials for priests and people. Now, new dimensions of "liturgical education" are opening up as we realize more clearly that discoveries of sociology and psychology, for instance, may be relevant to the question of how the Catholic people of today — in our great cities and their inner cities, in suburbs and rural areas — are *all* to come to "understand the sacred rites and take part in them fully, actively and as befits a community." No, the work of the Conference is not over; it is entering a new phase, in which it hopes to be of more service to the Church in America than it was able to be in the past. Perhaps this is a dream come true, but it is certainly not a *nunc dimittis*.

Quite a Way
To Go Yet

It is certainly very difficult, given the architecture of many churches, to implement the spirit as well as the letter of the changes in the liturgy. The long-and-narrow Gothic type of church building, for instance, was designed for a Mass thought of as something to be present at, not to take part in. The "new" idea, that the congregation should feel themselves to be gathered around the table of the Lord, will take quite a while to implement in every parish church.

It isn't a question of size or the number of people to be accommodated. Our parish church, for instance, is quite small, made out of an old New England house. The interior is almost square and the people are on three sides of the sanctuary. Now that the altar for Mass is out away from the wall, and the celebrant stands behind it, he really does look as though he were presiding at a gathering round a table. But the same effect was obtained at the Baltimore liturgical week in the vast Civic Center, as it has been at previous liturgical weeks in equally vast auditoriums, because the altar was set up to look like the center around which people are gathered. Maybe something could be done even with long and narrow church buildings, if somebody with imagination and the right idea were allowed to get at them. Something could, one would think, be done about pews, for instance. Surely they could be designed so that they don't seem to keep people apart, but rather gathered together in an orderly and reasonably comfortable way.

Even worse, of course, than a style of architecture that is fighting the changes is a celebrant who isn't "with" them. When one has to hear the Word of God read in English as if it really didn't mean anything and was just something to get through, when the priest faces the people but speaks and acts as if he were doing something very hush-hush all by himself that they are eavesdropping at, one is tempted to wish that he were celebrating the Mass the old way. The new letter seems worse than useless without the new spirit — and it is almost impossible for the people to have the new spirit if the celebrant doesn't.

Of course, the rites themselves at the present stage of reform aren't consistent in facilitating the new spirit either. It doesn't make any sense for the celebrant to lapse into Latin at all, if the people are really meant to be "in on" what he is saying and doing. Particularly when he is carrying out the great eucharistic prayer, in the course of which the celebrant acts "in the person of Christ," it doesn't make any sense for him to be speaking in Latin and in a "low tone." Our Lord certainly didn't speak in a dead language and under his breath at the Last Supper when he said, "This is my body. . . . This is my blood. . . ."

It doesn't make any sense, that is, according to the "new" idea of the Mass, set out in the *Constitution on the Sacred Liturgy,* which seems to be nearer to the New Testament idea than anything we have had for many centuries. But we have a long way to go to carry out the transformation the Church is determined to produce, of a Mass that had become fossilized as an "ancient rite" (however intense our personal devotion at it) into a Mass that will be a joyful personal and communal celebration of God's love accomplishing its wonderful works in our midst. We shall have to change our architecture, our music, our art and, above all, ourselves if the present and future reforms in the rites are to be effective.

But sometimes one can realize a little of what it will be like when all this is achieved. In our parish, for instance, and surely in many others throughout the country, we are blessed with priests who celebrate Mass as if they were really presiding at a gathering in which everyone was meant to be concerned with what is going on. At every Mass, the celebrant carries out the eucharistic prayer in such a way that we do not feel "included out" while he is going through mysterious rites on his own, but included in a gathering in which, through his visible ministry as celebrant, the Lord is carrying out what he did at the Last Supper so that we can be part of it. At such a Mass, one feels that we are on our way, that all the present is already proving worthwhile.